Masters: Glass Beads

MICHAEL BARLEY ■ DIANA EAST ■ TOM BOYLAN ■
TOSHIKI UCHIDA ■ PAM DUGGER ■ LEAH FAIRBANKS
■ ANDREA GUARINO-SLEMMONS ■ KRISTINA LOGAN ■
TOM HOLLAND ■ LARK DALTON AND CORRIE HAIGHT
■ BRUCE ST. JOHN MAHER ■ AKIHIRO OHKAMA ■
JIM SMIRCICH ■ KAREN OVINGTON ■ SHARON PETERS
■ YOSHIKO SHIIBA ■ KATE FOWLE MELENEY ■
NORIKAZU KOGURE ■ GAIL CROSMAN MOORE
■ MARY MULLANEY AND RALPH MOSSMAN ■

KRISTEN FRANTZEN ORR ■ TOSHIMASA MASUI ■
DONNA MILLIRON ■ HAROLD WILLIAMS COONEY
■ TERRI CASPARY SCHMIDT ■ PATI WALTON ■
RENÉ ROBERTS ■ HIROKO HAYASHI-KOGURE
■ LOREN STUMP ■ JAMES ALLEN JONES ■
SAGE HOLLAND ■ PAT FRANTZ ■ EMIKO SAWAMOTO ■
NICOLE ZUMKELLER AND ERIC SEYDOUX ■ DAN ADAMS
■ DAVIDE PENSO ■ DONI HATZ ■ SHIGEMICHI YAGI ■
BRONWEN HEILMAN ■ DUSTIN TABOR

Masters: Glass Beads

Major Works by Leading Artists

Curated by Larry Scott

LARK BOOKS
A Division of Sterling Publishing Co., Inc.
New York / London

SENIOR EDITOR:
Suzanne J. E. Tourtillott

EDITOR:
Larry Shea

ART DIRECTOR:
Megan Kirby

COVER DESIGNER:
Cindy LaBreacht

ASSISTANT EDITOR:
Shannon Quinn-Tucker

ASSOCIATE ART DIRECTOR:
Travis Medford

EDITORIAL ASSISTANCE:
Julie Hale and Mark Bloom

Library of Congress Cataloging-in-Publication Data

Masters. Glass beads : major works by leading artists / editor, Suzanne J.E. Tourtillott. -- 1st ed.
    p. cm.
  Includes index.
  ISBN-13: 978-1-57990-924-6 (pb-trade pbk. : alk. paper)
  ISBN-10: 1-57990-924-8 (pb-trade pbk. : alk. paper)
  1. Beadwork. 2. Glass beads. I. Tourtillott, Suzanne J. E. II. Title: Glass beads.
  NK5440.B34M37 2008
  748.8'5--dc22

                             2007041515

10 9 8 7 6 5 4 3 2 1

First Edition

Published by Lark Books, A Division of
Sterling Publishing Co., Inc.
387 Park Avenue South, New York, N.Y. 10016

Text © 2008, Lark Books
Photography © 2008, Artist/Photographer as specified

Distributed in Canada by Sterling Publishing,
c/o Canadian Manda Group, 165 Dufferin Street
Toronto, Ontario, Canada M6K 3H6

Distributed in the United Kingdom by GMC Distribution Services,
Castle Place, 166 High Street, Lewes, East Sussex, England BN7 1XU

Distributed in Australia by Capricorn Link (Australia) Pty Ltd.,
P.O. Box 704, Windsor, NSW 2756 Australia

If you have questions or comments about this book, please contact:
Lark Books
67 Broadway
Asheville, NC 28801
(828) 253-0467

Manufactured in China

ISBN 13: 978-1-57990-924-6
ISBN 10: 1-57990-924-8

For information about custom editions, special sales, premium and corporate purchases, please contact
Sterling Special Sales Department at 800-805-5489 or specialsales@sterlingpub.com.

Contents

Introduction

MASTERS: GLASS BEADS is a status report on the emerging craft of studio glass beadmaking.

While glass beadmaking has a long, if discontinuous, history stretching back to at least the ancient Egyptians, studio glass beadmaking, where the creator is both the designer and the maker, is a recent development. In the United States and Europe, it is barely 20 years old. In Japan, where craftsman beadmaking has a longer history, the last 20 years have taken beadmaking well beyond its traditional roots.

The primary reason for this rapid development, this Cambrian Explosion of glass beadmaking, is essentially coincidence. Starting in the 1980s, the availability of torches for scientific glassblowing, small kilns for ceramics, and colored glass rods made it possible to make glass beads in the small-scale studio. As humans have been making beads from just about anything at hand for the last 40,000 years, it is no surprise that studio glass beadmaking has been taken up by so many people, so quickly, and so enthusiastically.

Making sense of all this activity is difficult. When Suzanne Tourtillott at Lark Books asked me to choose 40 beadmakers for a volume in their Masters series, my first question was "What constitutes a 'Master' beadmaker?" There are no established training programs or serious apprenticeships for beadmakers. Most articles about beadmakers and their work are essentially promotional.

Despite the current popularity of books and magazines about beads and beadmaking, a critical vocabulary specific to beadmaking has been slow to develop. The adjectives "awesome" and "gorgeous" do not constitute thoughtful critical assessment.

In making selections for this book, I have taken the term "master" to be an honorary and decidedly casual title awarded by peers. It's as if over dinner and a glass of wine, a few accomplished beadmakers might concede that some absent colleague is a master. This is a broad but useful definition, which takes some of the ginger out of a potentially controversial appellation.

The glass beadmakers showcased here represent the sprawling diversity of subject matter, form, innovation, and technical mastery in contemporary beadmaking. Time does grant authority, and all of the artists in this book have produced a considerable and widely recognized body of work over years of beadmaking.

When making my selections, I tried to be as inclusive as possible. Basically, a studio glass bead is anything that meets three criteria: It's made of glass; it's made, hands on, by the designer; and it's made with a hole through it. The majority of the beads in this book have been flameworked on a torch. Others have been drawn out in a hot shop, fused in a kiln, or cold cast in molds. They have been painted, enameled, etched, sandblasted, carved, ground, and polished. They are shiny and matte, smooth and rough, representational and abstract, serious and funny, historically informed and blatantly modern, anthropological and mineralogical, botanical and zoological. They are, in turn, safe, subversive, refined, and blissfully uncouth.

The eight-page galleries in this collection contain photographs of at least 12 beads by each beadmaker. Some pictures include more than one bead of a similar style. In some cases, whole strands of nearly identical beads are shown. Some are shown in combination with other materials, such as polymer clay and felt. The majority are of single focal beads.

Each gallery is a solo exhibition presenting the finest examples of each beadmaker's work over time, with particular emphasis on those aspects of their work that marked them for inclusion here. Interspersed with the photographs are quotations from the beadmakers that offer insight into their approach to beadmaking, creative life, and personal philosophy. At the beginning of each gallery is an introduction which, in its brevity, can only hint at what makes the work notable.

Ultimately, I went about this project from a beadmaker's perspective. I have been a beadmaker myself, since February 13, 1993. For me it is an important date. I still have my first bead. I had no way of knowing then that my life would be made so full and so rich by so small a thing. All beadmakers would say the same.

—Larry Scott
Curator

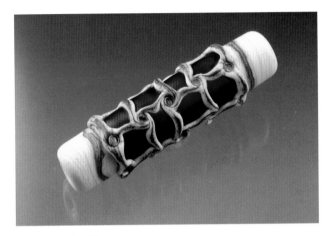

▲ Larry Scott
Red Window Bead | 2006

5.2 cm x 1.6 cm

Lampworked, heat and gravity shaped, textured, etched, dichroic coating; soda-lime glass

Photo by Andrea Guarino-Slemmons

Michael Barley

WHEN MICHAEL BARLEY SAYS that the sandstone canyons of Utah and the forests and beaches of the Pacific Northwest serve as inspiration for his work, viewers may find it difficult to see what he is talking about. There are no mesas, Douglas firs, or ocean breakers etched onto his beads. Yet the influence is undoubtedly there. The essence of the landscape has been distilled into his work.

Barley's beads feature twisted lines that resemble the strata on canyon walls or rivulets of water on an ocean beach. He uses layers of varied transparent colors in his beads to create the shifting hues of wet pebbles on a shoreline. Silver-lined windows give viewers the illusion that they are peering into his beads through the ripples on a lake. None of this happens by accident. Through restless experimentation with glass chemistry, enamel powders, metallic leaf, and silver fuming, Barley has amassed a formidable repertoire of effects. He exploits unexpected results to their fullest extent.

Untitled | 2006 ▶
4.9 x 2.2 cm
Lampworked; Effetre glass
Photo by Joanie Beldin

▲ Untitled | 2006

4.7 x 3.3 cm
Lampworked; Effetre glass
Photo by Joanie Beldin

▲ Untitled | 2006

2.9 x 2.9 cm
Lampworked; Effetre glass
Photo by Joanie Beldin

▲ **Untitled** | 2006

5 x 3.2 cm
Lampworked; Effetre glass
Photo by Joanie Beldin

" One of the things I find so appealing about beads is the limitation that their size sets for me. There is the practical issue of how large a bead can be and still be functional. The challenge is to work within these boundaries and continue to keep things interesting. "

▲ **Untitled** | 1998

3.8 x 2.2 cm
Lampworked; Moretti glass
Photo by Doug Yaple

▼ **Untitled** | 1996

45 cm long
Lampworked; Moretti glass
Photo by Doug Yaple

▲ **Untitled** | 2006

3.5 x 3.5 cm

Lampworked; Effetre glass

Photo by Joanie Beldin

Untitled | 2006 ▶

4 x 2 cm

Lampworked; Satake glass

Photo by Joanie Beldin

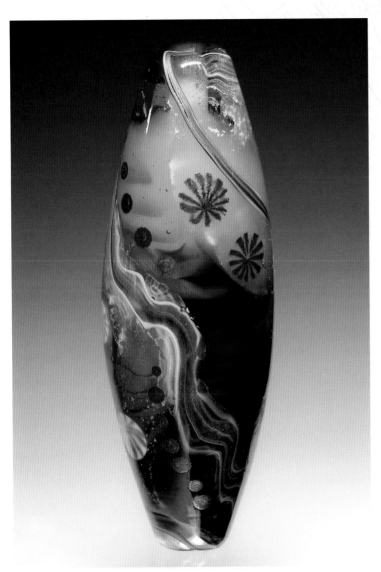

" I've lived in the Pacific Northwest for thirty years and spent a lot of time hiking in the mountains and on the beaches. I'm sure that my aesthetic sensibilities have developed because of these experiences. I like to blend glass to create subtle shifts in color and tone, similar to the way that fog or mist will change the landscape. "

◀ **Untitled** | 2006

4.9 x 2.1 cm
Lampworked; Satake glass
Photo by Joanie Beldin

▲ **Untitled** | 2006

4.8 x 1.9 cm
Lampworked; Effetre glass
Photo by Joanie Beldin

▼ **Untitled** | 1993

3.2 x 2.4 cm
Lampworked; Moretti glass
Photo by artist

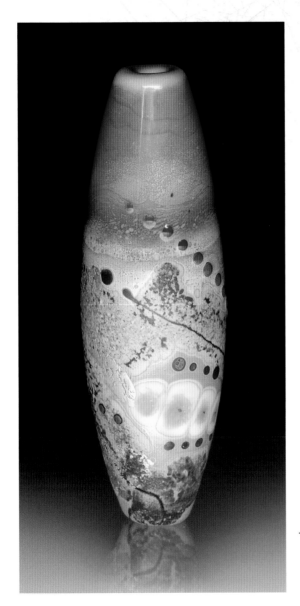

" Glass offers me immediate gratification.
It allows me to test a color combination,
and within seconds, I can look at the
results and proceed with the idea or not.
Another quality about glass that I find
alluring is its ability to be transparent.
This lets me layer colors in ways to
create new colors, offering me a palette
of infinite choices. "

◀ **Untitled** │ 2006

5.3 x 2 cm
Lampworked; Effetre glass
Photo by Joanie Beldinzz

MICHAEL BARLEY

Diana East

SANDBLASTING MAY SEEM like a crude technique for a bead maker to use, but for Diana East it provides a means of exploring the relationship between the inside and outside of her beads. East sandblasts almost the entire exterior of some of her pieces, so that the original surface remains only in windswept forms or in visions of the Arabian Nights. On other beads, small windows have been cut to reveal the interior. A look through the window may reveal a simple color or a complicated pattern.

Frequently, however, someone is looking back through the window. One of East's beads contains inhabitants that seem packed in a little too close for comfort, while another features figures that seem perfectly content. East uses sandblasting to cut into the bead, then adds small spheres of glass on steel rods to elevate the surface of the bead. These retro-modern pieces are colorful and diverting. They also display East's fine British sense of humor.

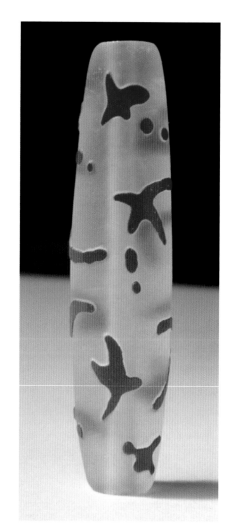

Marks | 2002 ▶
6 x 1 x .75 cm
Flameworked, layered, sandblasted;
Effetre glass, enamels
Photo by artist

Untitled | 2002 ▶

Dimensions and materials
unknown

Photo by artist

▲
Mosque | 1999

3 cm high, not including mount
Flameworked, layered, gold fumed, sandblasted, etched;
Effetre glass, enamels

Photo by artist

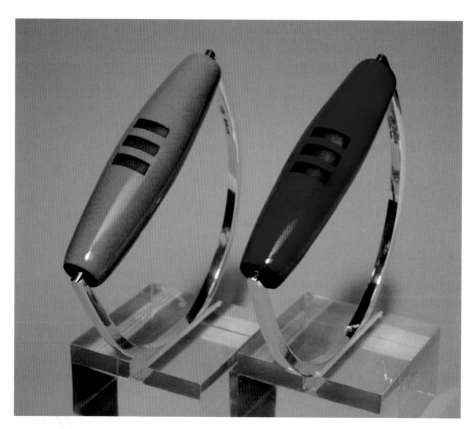

▲ **Two Silver Bracelets from the Grill Series** │ 2002

6 cm long
Flameworked, layered, sandblasted, fire polished;
Effetre glass, enamels

Photo by artist

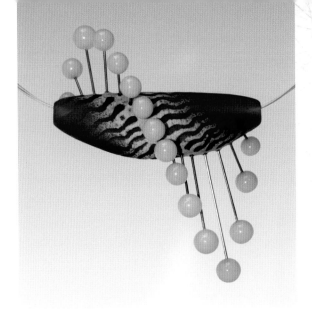

▲ **Ripple** | 2006

7 x 2.5 x 1.5 cm
Flameworked, mandrel wound, carved, sandblasted;
Effetre glass, enamel

Photo by Lucy Hunt

" I mainly make wearable pieces because I am interested

in how the wearing of a piece can alter one's

perception of self. **"**

▲ **Different Orbits** | 2005

7 cm long
Flameworked, mandrel wound, layered,
sandblasted, fire polished; Effetre glass,
enamels, murrini, stainless steel armatures
with cold-bonded finials

Photo by artist

▲ **Thoughts Float Like Clouds Above a Clear Blue Sea of Consciousness** | 2007

9 x 2.5 x 1.5 cm

Flameworked, mandrel wound, layered, carved, sandblasted, engraved; Effetre glass, dichroic glass, enamels

Photo by artist

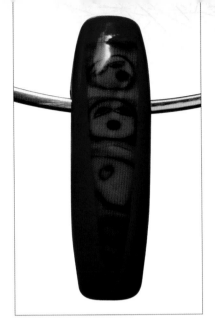

" After working for over twenty years as a freelance jewelry designer/maker, I began working in glass in 1995. I've found that glass is a wonderful medium for personal expression, and I've been able to help introduce other people to it through teaching the technique of flamework. "

▲ It's Easy to Get Drawn Into the Argument | 2002

6 x 1 x 0.5 cm
Flameworked, mandrel wound, layered, sandblasted, fire polished; Effetre glass, murrini, enamels
Photo by artist

Chain Reaction and Loop | 2004 ▶

7 cm tall
Flameworked, mandrel wound, layered, sandblasted; Effetre glass, enamels, stainless steel armatures with cold-bonded finials
Photo by artist

" I find it amazing and fascinating that consciousness is an electro-chemical process, and that perception is entirely virtual, being processed by the brain. I try to visualize these facts through my work in glass. "

◀ **3 Decorative Beads** | 2000

3 cm long
Flameworked, gold fumed, clear cased,
dot decoration; Effetre glass, enamels

Photo by artist

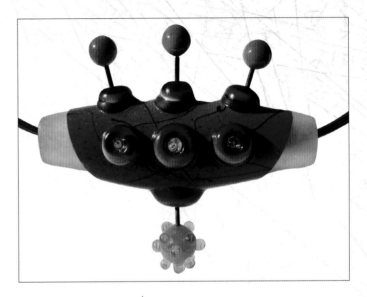

▲ **Action Potential** | 2003

4. 4 cm long
Flameworked, mandrel wound, Effetre glass, stainless steel armatures with cold-bonded finials

Photo by artist

▲ **Moonlit Ruins** | 2000

3 cm high, not including mount
Flameworked, mandrel wound, layered, gold fumed, sandblasted, etched; Effetre glass, dichroic glass, frit, enamels

Photo by artist

DIANA EAST

Tom Boylan

TOM BOYLAN IS LARGELY A SELF-TAUGHT BEAD MAKER, a fact that he has used to his advantage. Not having a teacher, he found, brought him all kinds of opportunities—chances for conceptual breakthroughs and technical roadblocks, brilliant designs and bad habits. Finding a way around those bad habits often led to new ideas.

Boylan makes his flameworked beads from the kind of borosilicate tubing typically used for scientific glassblowing. To make a bead, he adds colored stripes and dots to the outside of one section of the tube—the part that will become the finished bead. The end of the tube near this section is temporarily closed off, so that the glass can be mouth-blown to increase the size or change the shape of the piece. Repeated heating of the colors produces different shades and levels of opacity. Boylan's meticulous technique, combined with his understanding of the chemistry of glass, produces regularity of color and pattern in each bead. As a final flourish, he adds a characteristic twist at each end of the bead.

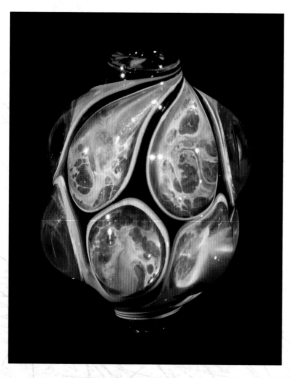

◀ **Untitled** | 1985

3 x 2.5 x 2.5 cm
Lampworked and blown, heat and gravity
shaped; borosilicate glass
Photo by John Birchard

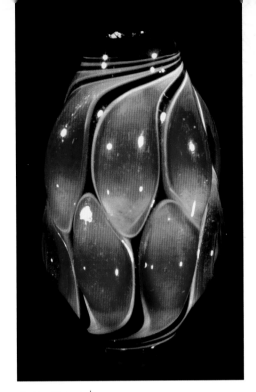

▲ **Untitled** | 1986

3.5 x 2 x 2 cm
Lampworked and blown, heat and gravity
shaped; borosilicate glass

Photo by John Birchard

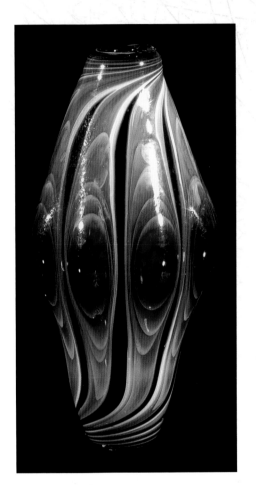

▲ **Untitled** | 1990

5 x 2.2 x 2.2 cm
Lampworked and blown, heat and gravity
shaped; borosilicate glass

Photo by John Birchard

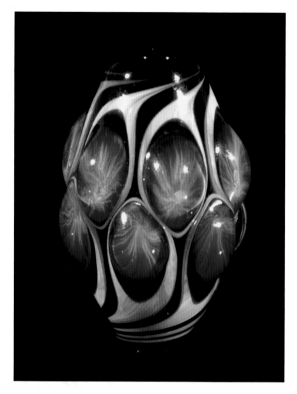

▲ **Untitled** │ 1996

3.5 x 2.5 x 2.5 cm
Lampworked and blown, heat and gravity
shaped; borosilicate glass

Photo by John Birchard

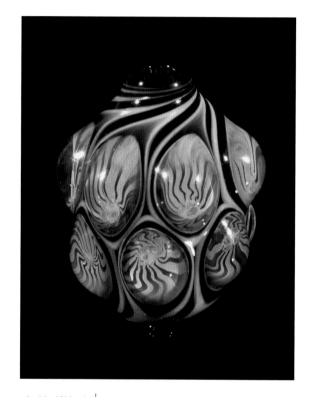

▲ **Untitled** │ 1998

3.5 x 2.5 x 2.5 cm
Lampworked and blown, heat and gravity
shaped; borosilicate glass

Photo by John Birchard

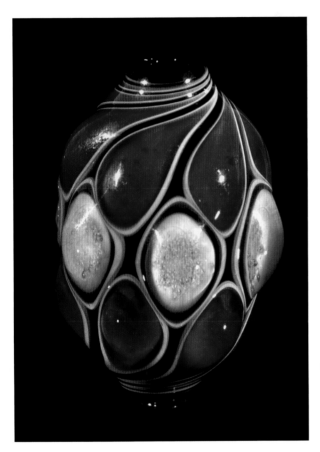

" What fascinates me about glass is that it is made from sand, the most common material in the crust of the earth. We, as artists, impose upon this common stuff our dreams, visions, and inspirations. We transform this common material until it becomes something that it would not have evolved into throughout the duration of the universe. "

◀ Untitled | 1994

4 x 2.5 x 2.5 cm
Lampworked and blown, heat and gravity
shaped; borosilicate glass

Photo by John Birchard

TOM BOYLAN

▲ **Untitled** | 1998
4.5 x 3.5 x 3.5 cm
Lampworked and blown, heat and gravity shaped;
borosilicate glass
Photo by John Birchard

" I have a love-hate relationship with glass.
Each day, I crave to walk away from it and
never return. But each day, I am drawn
back to it. Glass is very physical. Hot
glass sags under the force of gravity, so
movement and timing come into play. The
process of glassblowing is like dancing with
a fire-breathing dragon. "

▲ **Untitled** | 1998

5 x 3.5 x 3.5 cm
Lampworked and blown, heat and gravity
shaped; borosilicate glass

Photo by John Birchard

▼ **Penny's Bead** | 1998

4.5 x 2.8 x 2.8 cm
Lampworked and blown, heat and gravity
shaped; borosilicate glass

Photo by John Birchard

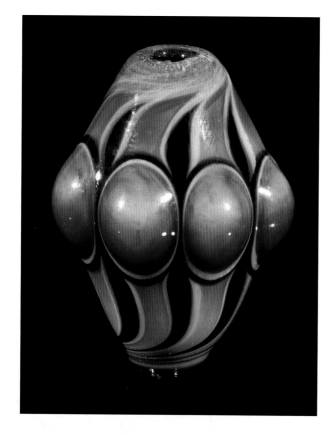

◀ **Untitled** | 2003

3.5 x 2.5 x 2.5 cm
Lampworked and blown, heat and gravity
shaped; borosilicate glass
Photo by John Birchard

" I like the idea that the art we bead makers create is not hidden away in some
vault or museum but is worn in the open, as adornment for all to see and
appreciate. I am thrilled when people tell me that whenever they wear my
beads, people stop them to ask questions and make comments. "

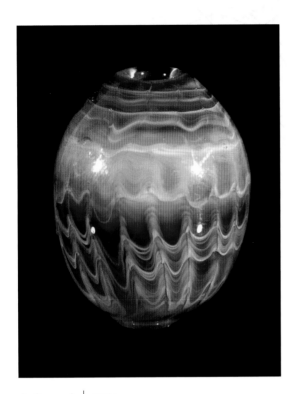

▲ **Sunset** | 2004

3.5 x 2.7 x 2.7 cm
Lampworked and blown, heat and gravity
shaped; borosilicate glass

Photo by John Birchard

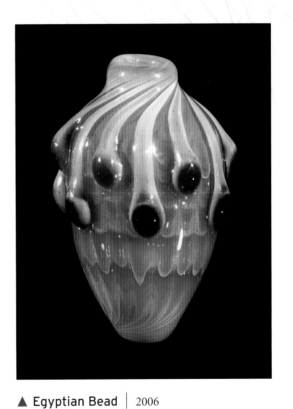

▲ **Egyptian Bead** | 2006

4 x 2.8 x 2.8 cm
Lampworked and blown, heat and gravity shaped;
borosilicate glass

Photo by John Birchard

Toshiki Uchida

TOSHIKI UCHIDA'S BEADS ARE SPHERICAL for the sake of practicality: a round bead is less likely to break. But that's where the practical traits of Uchida's beads end, and the improbable qualities begin. The intricacy of his minute mosaic patterns creates an effect that is like being in a hall of mirrors. Forms echo forms in shape and design from every angle. His beads are like never-ending Persian carpets laid out in curved space.

   Uchida uses small mosaic segments to form the leaflets of ferns and the feathery petals of flowers. He combines these tiny segments to create a full fern leaf or flower that he will insert into a bead. Uchida also positions individual canes that have been twisted clockwise and counterclockwise side by side, so that they form leaves with sharply angled veins. Repetition and invention, the practical and the improbable—Uchida has the skill to combine all of these qualities in a single bead.

Hebiichigo Flower | 2000 ▶

2.2 x 2.2 x 2.2 cm
Lampworked; lead glass, hand-made murrini, handmade cane
Photo by artist

◄ **Flora** │ 2000

2.3 x 2.3 x 2.3 cm
Lampworked; lead glass,
handmade twisted cane

Photo by artist

Fossil │ 1997 ►

1.7 x 1.7 x 1.7 cm
Lampworked; lead glass,
soda-lime glass

Photo by artist

Flora | 2001 ▶
2.2 x 2 x 2 cm
Lampworked; lead glass,
handmade cane
Photo by artist

" Things like cracks in the
sidewalk, a grass vine, or a
piece of rusty iron sometimes
appear to have unique patterns.
Most of the ideas of my work
come from things like these—
objects that we often see in our
everyday life. I concentrate on
expressing the atmosphere or
the impression of the object
rather than reproducing the
object itself precisely. "

◀ **Flora** | 2001
2.4 x 2.4 x 2.4 cm
Lampworked; lead glass, handmade murrini,
handmade cane
Photo by artist

TOSHIKI UCHIDA

▲ **Jellyfish** | 2001

2 x 2 x 2 cm
Lampworked; lead glass, handmade murrini, handmade cane

Photo by artist

◀ **Peacock** │ 1999

2.3 x 2 x 2 cm
Lampworked; lead glass, handmade murrini, ground surface

Photo by artist

◀ **Untitled** │ 2002

1.6 x 1.6 x 1.6 cm
Lampworked; lead glass, soda-lime glass, hand-made twisted cane

Photo by artist

" I give myself over to making glass beads every day now. It's great fun to be in the process of designing, repeating much trial and error in front of the torch, and finally achieving the thing I picture in my mind. "

▲ Karasuuri Flower | 1994

2.3 x 2.3 x 2.3 cm
Lampworked; lead glass, handmade murrini
Photo by artist

" A glass bead is a small, round thing that is a clipping out of a certain scene or world. You can take it along anywhere you go. You can hold it in your hand and enjoy looking at it anytime you want. That's how I would like people to enjoy glass beads. "

▲ **Green Mosaic** | 2005

1.8 x 2.2 x 2.2 cm
Lampworked; leadglass, handmade murrini
Photo by artist

Mosaic | 2003 ▶

2.4 x 1.7 x 1.7 cm
Lampworked; lead
glass, handmade
murrini
Photo by artist

▲ **Ancient Flower** | 2002

2.2 x 2.2 x 2.2 cm
Lampworked; lead glass, handmade murrini, handmade cane
Photo by artist

Pam Dugger

A HOLLOW BEAD SERVES AS A STARTING POINT for Pam Dugger. As a lighter version of a typical flameworked bead, a hollow bead provides a good base for her larger-scale beads. The basic procedure for creating a hollow bead involves making two widely separated thin disk beads on one mandrel. The edges of the disks are then marvered toward each other until they touch. Once the disks are sealed all around, the air trapped inside them expands and puffs the bead out into a spherical shape.

Hollow beads refract and transmit light differently than solid glass beads. The beads add a lively transparency to Dugger's fish and bird beads. Using the fish body as a canvas has allowed Dugger to concentrate on color reactions and the endless patterns that are attainable when working with glass. She achieves intricate patterns of color and shape for each fish through the inventive layering of opaque and transparent colors over the initial hollow bead.

◀ **Clown Fish** │ 2004

8.9 x 3.8 x 7.6 cm
Mandrel-wound hollow bead; shaped, cased, sculpted, decorated; soda-lime glass

Photo by Jerry Anthony

▲ **Golden Wrasse** | 2005

7.6 x 7.6 x 7.6 cm
Mandrel-wound hollow bead; shaped, cased,
sculpted; applied scales, luster-type soda-lime
glass
Photo by Jerry Anthony

◀ **Lion Fish** | 2001

7.6 x 5.1 x 7.6 cm
Mandrel-wound hollow bead;
shaped, cased; sculpted, cut; soda-
lime glass

Photo by Jeffrey O'Dell

▲ **Panther Grouper** | 2001

8.9 x 2.5 x 5.1 cm
Mandrel-wound hollow bead, shaped, cased,
sculpted; soda-lime glass

Photo by Jeffrey O'Dell

◀ **Saddled Rock-Cod** | 2001

7.6 x 2.5 x 3.8 cm
Mandrel-wound hollow bead; shaped, cased,
sculpted, decorated; soda-lime glass

Photo by Jeffrey O'Dell

" The day I discovered hollow glass beads, my fate was sealed. The movement of the glass encapsulating a pocket of air intrigues me. I have painted glass, fused it, blown it, made paperweights from it, but I always came back to the miniature universe of beads, where I strive to project my thoughts into this glowing, molten, lava-like medium. "

▲ **Untitled** │ 2005

45.7 cm long
Lampworked; applied decorations,
luster glass, soda-lime glass

Photo by Jerry Anthony

▲ **St. Lucia Parrot** │ 2001

7.6 x 2.5 x 2.5 cm
Mandrel-wound hollow bead; shaped, cased,
sculpted; soda-lime glass, applied feathers
Photo by Jeffrey O'Dell

▲ **Regal Tang** │ 1995

3.8 cm long
Mandrel-wound hollow bead; soda-lime glass
Photo by artist

" Every time I sit at my bench and turn on my torch, it's a new adventure into the world of glass. Glass captivates me with its constant challenge and transparent beauty. Glass has a tremendous capacity—for what can be done with it, where you can go with it, where it can take you. "

▲ **Untitled** | 2005

    50.8 cm long
    Lampworked; applied decorations,
    luster glass, soda-lime glass

    Photo by Jerry Anthony

" We are at the tip of the iceberg in finding techniques and materials for working with glass. Making glass beads takes concentration, planning, the ability to change directions at the whim of the glass, and the idea that perfection is not achievable. If I were able to make the perfect bead, I would quit. There would be no challenge left. "

▲ **Orange Epaulette Surgeonfish** | 2001
8.9 x 2.5 x 7.6 cm
Mandrel-wound hollow bead; shaped, cased, sculpted; soda-lime glass
Photo by Jerry Anthony

◄ **Spotted Hawkfish** | 1995
3.8 cm long
Mandrel-wound hollow bead; soda-lime glass
Photo by artist

▲ **Ocean Triggerfish** | 2004

7.6 x 2.5 x 7.6 cm
Mandrel-wound hollow bead; shaped,
cased, sculpted, decorated; silver, copper,
and gold leaf, soda-lime glass
Photo by Jerry Anthony

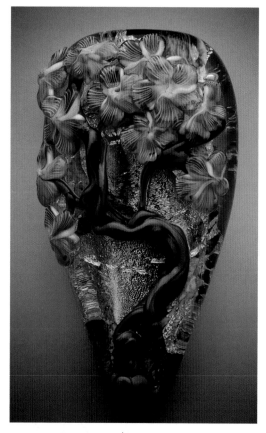

Leah Fairbanks

LIKE AN ENGLISH COTTAGE GARDEN, Leah Fairbanks' floral beads overflow with color and abundance. While the flower types are easily identifiable on her beads, Fairbanks' depictions are more like impressions of flowers rather than strict botanical illustrations.

Fairbanks achieves the complexity of branches, leaves, and blossoms on each bead by using ribbed canes and thin glass elements called coated stringers. The flowers ride high on the surface of a base bead, which is usually vase-shaped. The base bead is built up in layers. A central core is decorated with dichroic glass, enamels, or metal leaf, and then encased with transparent glass complementary to the floral design. Fairbanks then uses the coated stringers and ribbed canes to "paint" flowers on to the surface of the bead. The designs are left raised. They are melted in only enough to keep them attached to the bead. In some of her beads, small gemstones in gold bezels are set into the center of the flowers.

▲ **Azalea Bonsai** | 2001
5.7 x 3.2 x 1.3 cm
Lampworked, heat and paddle shaped; cased canes, dichroic glass, gold foil, soda-lime glass
Photo by George Post

FAIRBANKS

▲ Bonsai Hawthorn Berries | 2001

5.1 x 3.2 x 1.9 cm
Lampworked, heat and paddle shaped; cased
canes, glass powders, dichroic glass, gold foil,
soda-lime glass

Photo by George Post

" Working directly in the flame with the molten glass is mesmerizing and magical. Lampworking requires your full attention. The process for me is an opportunity to be completely suspended in the moment. I continually strive to refine my lampwork techniques to expand the visual depth in my beads. It's all about the layers. "

▲ **Multi-Colored Gladiolus #2** | 2001

5.7 x 2.5 x 1.3 cm
Lampworked, heat and paddle shaped;
cased canes, gold foil, glass enamels, soda-
lime glass, glass frit

Photo by George Post

▲ **High Bush Cranberries** | 2000

6.4 x 1.9 x 1.9 cm
Lampworked, heat and paddle shaped; cased
canes, glass enamels, gold and silver foil,
soda-lime glass

Photo by George Post

" My palettes are influenced by the changing seasons. These are the elements I strive to recreate in glass. I like to think of glass rods as tubes of paint. My goal is to blend the colors, then paint with them using my bead as the canvas. Color blending and experimentation have been crucial to my development as an artist. "

◀ **Autumn Floral** | 2006

5.7 x 2.5 x 1.9 cm
Lampworked, heat and paddle shaped; applied cased canes, glass fruit; gold foil, 18k gem sets, soda-lime glass

Photo by Derek Lusk

LEAH **FAIRBANKS**

" Inspiration flows from everyday experience. A diaphanous piece of fabric or the patterns of needles on a forest floor can inspire a series of beads. The intricate details of flowers and landscapes hold infinite possibilities for bead making. I am fascinated by the transformation of glass from a solid rod into liquid form, and by the reflections of glass and gems. "

▲ **Azalea Branches, Master Series** │ 2006
8.3 x 2.5 x 2.5 cm
Lampworked, paddle shaped; applied cased canes, gold foil, dichroic glass, gem set; soda-lime glass
Photo by Derek Lusk

▲ **Purple Gladiolus** | 2001

7.6 x 1.9 x 1.9 cm
Lampworked; heat and paddle shaped; cased
canes, glass enamels, silver and gold foil, soda-
lime glass

Photo by George Post

▲ **Multi-Colored Iris Medallion** | 2000

3.8 x 2.5 x 1.3 cm
Lampworked, heat and paddle shaped;
cased canes, glass enamels, gold leaf

Photo by George Post

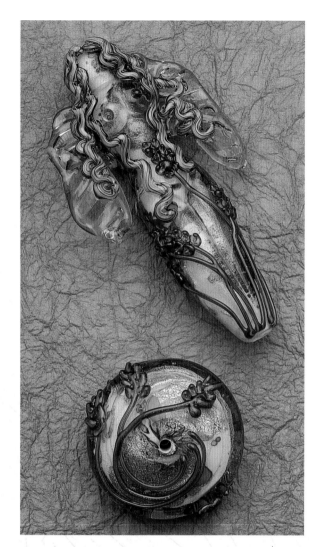

▲ **Winged Wheat Goddess & Wheat Lentil** │ 1998

Goddess: 8.9 x 5.1 x 1.9 cm; lentil: 5.1 x 5.1 x 1.3 cm
Lampworked, heat and paddle shaped; dichroic glass,
palladium leaf, glass frits, cased cane decoration, clear
soda-lime glass, latticino

Photo by George Post

▲ **Purple Plum Blossoms** │ 2000

6.4 x 2.5 x 2.5 cm
Lampworked, heat and paddle shaped; cased
canes, glass frit, gold foil; soda-lime glass

Photo by George Post

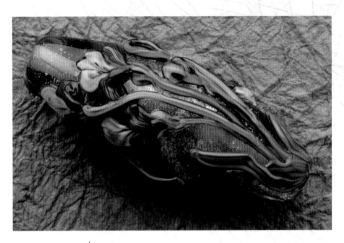

▲ **Untitled** | 1997

6.4 x 1.9 x 1.9 cm
Lampworked, heat and paddle shaped; palladium,
dichroic glass, cased canes, soda-lime glass

Photo by George Post

▲ **Daffodil Goddess** | 1996

7.6 x 5.7 x 1.9 cm
Lampworked, heat and paddle shaped; latticino,
glass enamels, cased cane decorations, soda-lime
glass

Photo by George Post

Andrea Guarino-Slemmons

LIKE MANY BEAD MAKERS, ANDREA GUARINO-SLEMMONS came to the craft after working with stained glass. Her early beads are neatly divided into separate panels and rigorously ordered patterns, like traditional leaded windows. Over time, her precision dot work gave way to swirling sea forms and intergalactic designs. Beads made on a stainless steel mandrel have now been joined by freer forms made on the end of a punty.

Silver plays a role in most of Guarino-Slemmons' beads. She melts silver wire to form the planets in some of her pieces. She uses volatilized silver and gold fuming to create warm hues of antique ivory. In some of her beads, silver salts resemble the mottled patterns of moth wings. Many beads are etched and waxed to a lustrous matte finish. Others are ground or faceted on lapidary equipment to reveal hidden interior designs.

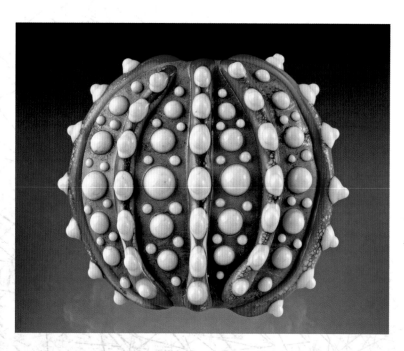

◀ **Sea Urchin** │ 2003
3.9 x 4.6 x 1.9 cm
Lampworked, marvered; applied stripes and dots, silver, soda-lime glass
Photo by artist

▲ **Hedge Hog** | 1995

4.4 x 2.4 cm
Lampworked, marvered; silver foil,
applied dots, soda-lime glass

Photo by artist

**" I love to manipulate glass by extending it
from the original bead surface and cutting
it to form different shapes like hearts,
feathers, wings, or leaves. The use of
lapidary equipment has opened up new
design possibilities. It allows me to open
windows to reveal interesting designs
inside my beads. "**

Moth Wing | 1999 ▶

3.7 x 3.8 x 1.4 cm
Lampworked, marvered; fumed with silver,
soda-lime glass

Photo by artist

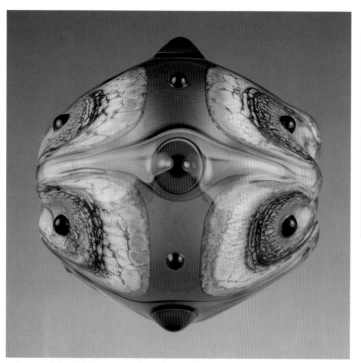

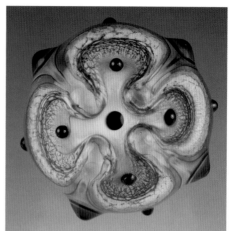

▲ **Blue Eyed Moth Wing** | 1999

2.9 x 3 cm
Lampworked, marvered; fumed with silver, applied dots
and feathering; soda-lime glass

Photos by artist

" The permanence of glass beads
amazes me. It's incredible to
think that hundreds of years
from now, even without special
care, these beads will still look
the same! Not many art forms
can make that statement. "

▲ **Ice Crystals** | 2005

   3 x 1.6 cm
   Lampworked, marvered; fumed with gold
   and silver, soda-lime glass

   Photo by artist

▲ **Sea Garden** | 2001

   4 x 4.1 x 1.5 cm
   Lampworked; applied dichroic and silver leaf,
   soda-lime glass

   Photo by artist

▼ **Galaxy Bead** | 2000

3.8 x 3.9 x 1.5 cm
Lampworked; silver leaf, silver fuming
and fine silver wire, soda-lime glass

Photos by artist

▲ **Flower Dot Bead** | 1994

2 x 2.7 cm
Lampworked, heat and gravity shaped;
manipulated dots, soda-lime glass

Photo by artist

▲ **Galaxy Within** | 2002

3.6 x 3 x 1.8 cm

Lampworked; fumed with silver, applied dots, twisted canes, soda-lime glass

Photo by artist

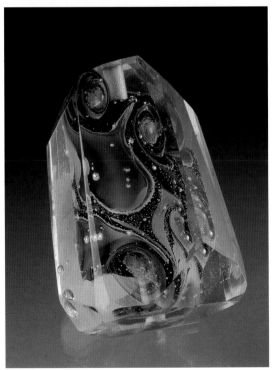

◄ **Galaxy Crystal** | 2004

3.5 x 2.7 x 1.6 cm

Lampworked, faceted; soda-lime glass

Photos by artist

◀ **Heart of Life** │ 2006

5.8 x 5.5 x .8 cm
Lampworked; enamels, soda-lime glass
Photos by artist

▲ **Egyptian Spiral** | 2006

5.9 x 1.9 cm
Lampworked; enamels; soda-lime
glass
Photo by artist

" I have blown glass on many
occasions and am excited by the
surface decoration techniques
that glass blowers use. A number
of my glass bead designs evolve
from these techniques. The
spiral is my very favorite design
element. Spirals appear on many
of my beads as raised, flat, tapered
or uniform designs, as well as
positive or negative spaces. "

Kristina Logan

THE DOT IS AN ESSENTIAL ELEMENT of design in glass bead making. A bead with four dots on it can reasonably be called a "dot" bead. But the beads of Kristina Logan—pieces with dozens or hundreds of precisely placed dots—are another type of bead entirely.

The surface of each of Logan's beads is completely covered with the pattern. Some of her pieces resemble mosaic floors or the stone pavements of Venice. Others resemble fragments of decorative molding from a Renaissance palace. Logan's beads make novelty seem overrated. They are evocative, but their exact references are far from clear. No matter how complex the pattern, her beads are essentially simple—one dot after another, peaceful and steady.

◀ **Amber Beads** | 1995

Tall bead: 4 x 3 x 3 cm
Lampworked, surface decorated;
soda-lime glass

Photo by artist

" The first time I saw someone flameworking, I had a feeling of excitement and shock. I was amazed that one could work glass independently, without the support of a studio. That is when I began experimenting and finding my own way with glass. Working glass at the torch, on such an intimate scale, gave me a sense of freedom and independence. "

◀ Olive Cactus Bead | 1997

4.5 x 4.2 x 2 cm
Lampworked, surface decorated; soda-lime glass
Photo by Paul Avis

◀ **Persian Disk Bead** | 2007

    1.2 x 4.5 x 4.5 cm
    Lampworked, surface decorated;
    soda-lime glass

    Photo by Paul Avis

◀ **Hollow Beads** | 2001

    5 x 5 x 5 cm
    Lampworked, surface deco-
    rated; soda-lime glass

    Photo by Paul Avis

▲ Disk Beads | 2006

Largest: 5.5 x 1.5 x 1.5 cm
Lampworked, surface decorated;
soda-lime glass

Photo by Dean Powell

" I have always thought of beads as sculptural objects for the human body. I am a sculptor by training, and that training has been invaluable to how I make beads today. That background has helped me take my thoughts and ideas and form them into three-dimensional objects."

KRISTINA LOGAN

▲ Ivory Totem Beads | 2003

    7.3 x 1.9 x 1.9 cm
Lampworked, surface decorated; soda-lime glass

Photo by Paul Avis

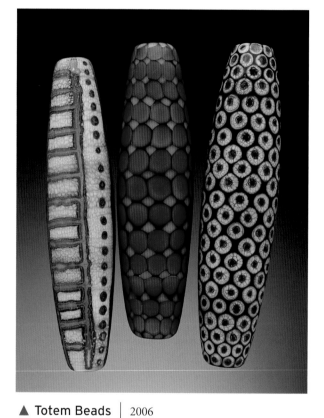

▲ Totem Beads | 2006

    10 x 2 x 2 cm
Lampworked, surface decorated; soda-lime glass

Photo by Dean Powell

▲ Ivory Disk | 2003

    1.3 x 5.4 x 5.4 cm
    Lampworked, surface decorated;
    soda-lime glass
    Photo by Paul Avis

Turquoise Cactus Bead | 1998 ▶

4.7 x 4 x 1.5 cm
Lampworked, surface decorated;
soda-lime glass

Photo by Paul Avis

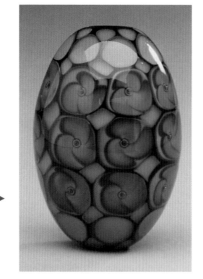

▲ **First Raised Dots** | 1992

2 x 2.5 x 2.5 cm
Lampworked, surface decorated; soda-lime glass
Photo by artist

▲ **Floral Bead** | 1993

2.5 x 1.8 x 1.8 cm
Lampworked, surface decorated; soda-lime glass
Photo by artist

" My patterns, color development, and precision are a result of years of experimentation. Architectural details, Renaissance and pre-Renaissance mosaics, and religious reliquaries from the 1300s and 1500s influence my work. I use glass beads as a base for all my work and as part of a connection to other people, past and present. "

▲ Barrel Beads | 2006

3.5 x 3 x 3 cm
Lampworked, surface decorated;
soda-lime glass

Photo by Dean Powell

Lark Dalton and Corrie Haight

FURNACE GLASS BEAD MAKING in a glass blower's hot shop is always a partnership. For Lark Dalton and Corrie Haight of Olive Glass, teamwork is essential—both in bead making and in raising a family. Like other furnace glass beads, theirs begin as long colored or striped tubes of glass that have been pulled in the hot shop. While some of these tubes are simply cut into bead-length pieces and tumble-polished, others are extensively coldworked.

Many of the pieces made by Dalton and Haight are hand-faceted. This technique adds liveliness to beads with simple, colored cores. During the bead-making process, Dalton and Haight sometimes reheat pieces of tube and introduce them to a torch in order to create tapered ends, or to tug the tubes into pillow shapes. The sections with larger diameters that come from the ends of the long tubes are reheated and twisted into puzzle knots or allowed to droop into simple curves.

◀ Pillows │ 1985

Largest: 2.5 x 3 x 1 cm
Handblown blank; lampworked,
shaped; soda-lime glass

Photo by Lark Tobin Dalton

▲ **Handblown Furnace Glass Beads** | 1984–2006

Largest: 3.8 x 1.3 cm
Handblown, cut, polished, layered; soda-lime glass
Photo by Lark Tobin Dalton

▲ **Large Full Spectrum Oval Beads** | 2000

2 x 6.5 x 1 cm
Handblown, flattened, layered; soda-lime glass
Photo by Lark Tobin Dalton

" It is exciting to be involved in an art that is ancient and ageless. Yet everything that comes from it is new. The idea that beads have survived the civilizations they were created in is fascinating. We like to think that some beads and designs from Olive Glass will be here after we are long gone. "

▲ **Aqua, Amethyst, and Green Rope Optic Curve** | 2006
    6.5 x 12.5 x 1 cm
    Handblown, heat and gravity shaped, layered; soda-lime glass
    Photo by Lark Tobin Dalton

◀ **Full Spectrum Squiggles** | 2002
    4 x 8 x 4 cm
    Handblown, heat and gravity shaped; soda-lime glass
    Photo by Lark Tobin Dalton

◀ **Handblown Tapered Silver Bracelet** | 1998
6.5 x 7 x 2.5 cm
Handblown, heat shaped, tapered, annealed, cut,
tumble polished; soda-lime glass
Photo by Lark Tobin Dalton

" Glass working is the balance of your center with the
movement and freezing of the molten glass. Without
the center, the glass is on its own. Because the technical
part of glass melting is so demanding, it's always great
to get to the part of the process that involves working
the glass in its hot state and creating new ideas. "

▲ **3-Piece Oval Ruby Aurora Bracelet Set** | 2000

6 x 8 x 2 cm
Handblown, heat and gravity shaped with mandrel; soda-lime glass

Photo by Lark Tobin Dalton

Gold, Ruby, and Purple Handfaceted Bead | 1994 ▶

5 x 1 x 1 cm
Handblown, hand faceted, layered; soda-lime glass

Photo by Lark Tobin Dalton

▲ **Handfaceted Beads** | 1990–2006

Largest: 2.5 x 1.3 cm
Handblown, hand faceted, layered, polished; soda-lime glass
Photo by Lark Tobin Dalton

" Our ability to be creative and exchange ideas together has allowed our designs to move forward to new levels of color and form. We think two heads are better than one. The hot glass shop, with its intense noise and heat, the teamwork and skill, the sharing of ideas—all this makes it easy to come back day after day. "

Large Purple and Aqua Optic Bead | 1996 ▶

5 x 3 x 5 cm
Handblown; soda-lime glass
Photo by Lark Tobin Dalton

▲ **Handblown Dichroic Sculpted Curve** │ 2006

    4 x 10 x 1.5 cm

    Handblown, tooled; applied dichroic coating, soda-lime glass

    Photo by Lark Tobin Dalton

Large Aqua Handblown Bead │ 1994 ▶

    5 x 8 x 5 cm

    Handblown, layered; soda-lime glass

    Photo by Lark Tobin Dalton

Bruce St. John Maher

▲ **Cubic Landscape/Blue** | 2004

3.5 x 1.2 cm
Kiln cast, layered, hand cut, fire polished;
enamel

Photo by George Reding

IN THE FUSED BEADS OF Bruce St. John Maher, the redwood forests of Northern California are held like fossils in some crystalline relative of amber. Using enamels, Maher paints forest scenes for his beads with precision and detail. A career in the restoration and reproduction of enameled stained glass prepared him for this work in miniature landscapes.

To make a bead, Maher encases a painted scene between enameled layers, dichroic glass, and a final, top layer of clear glass. The stack of glass is then fused in a kiln. Maher fine-tunes his shapes through hand lapidary work and faceting. A typical Maher bead features a small enameled fly encased in topaz glass with faceted edges—a piece that resembles amber from some Baltic beach.

▲ **Landscape with Opal Moon** | 2004

5 x 2 cm
Fused; enamel, frit; Australian opal, luminous phosphors
Photo by Patrick Craig

▲ **Faux Amber/Housefly** | 2005

4 x 4 cm
Fused, coldworked,
fire polished; enamel
Photo by George Reding

▲ **Lovers Tokens/Gold Mountain Series** | 1998

4 x 4 cm

Fused, hand cut, fire polished; enamel

Photo by Janice Peacock

▲ **Red Sullivan** | 1996

4 x 3 cm

Encased, coldworked, fire polished,
tempered; multi-stage enamel

Photo by Janice Peacock

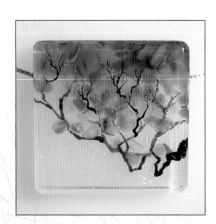

◀ **Large Cherry Tree** | 1998

4 x 4 cm

Coldworked, fire polished;
frits, enamels

Photo by Janice Peacock

MAHER

BRUCE ST. JOHN

" The domino shape refers to both scroll painting and a window frame. With this format, I can play with lots of different materials and techniques in small editions. I get the freedom to fail. "

▲ **Assorted Cherry Trees** │ 1998–1999

4 x 2 to 5.5 x 2 cm
Layered, coldworked, fire polished; enamels, frits
Photo by Robert Liu

" After a lifetime of coloring and melting glass, I still have a hard time going to bed with the anticipation of what's cooling down. Luckily, epiphanies seem more common in the wee hours. "

▲ Optic/Blue Base │ 2000

3.3 x 2.7 cm
Tack fused, coldworked, fire polished;
dichro/soda-lime glass
Photo by Robert Liu

▲ Rainbow Dangle Strand │ 1998

Each: 2 x .7 cm; strand: 45.7 cm long
Fusion in two pieces
Photo by Janice Peacock

▲ **Assorted Bull's Eye Optics** | 2000

1.5 x 3 cm to 4 x 3 cm
Tack fused, coldworked, shaped, textured; dichroic glass

Photo by Robert Liu

" Making a series of matching beads is always a ritual. When it's done well, it becomes a meditation. "

▲ **Rainbow Scarab Strand** │ 1998

Each: 1.5 x 2.5 cm; strand: 45.7 cm long
Fused in four pieces

Photo by Janice Peacock

▲ Assorted Bracelets | 2000

    4 x 8 x 8 cm
    Kiln cast, hand-cut, fire polished,
    tempered; dichro/soda-lime glass;

    Photo by Robert Liu

Akihiro Ohkama

▲ **Cherry Blossom and Moon** | 2003

2 x 1.8 x 1.8 cm
Lampworked; pixie dust, murrini, Satake
glass, soda-lime glass

Photo by artist

AMONG JAPANESE BEADMAKERS, Akihiro Ohkama has
become something of a crossover artist. His work reflects his
Japanese heritage, but it also has strong Western qualities. Most
of Ohkama's beads are made on a Japanese upright torch with soft
glass. The bead shape is the common short barrel. The surface
designs and patterns—delicate cherry blossoms and hibiscus—are
unmistakably those of a Japanese bead maker.

Other beads reflect Western culture and the paperweight
tradition. In some of Ohkama's pieces, flowers are deeply encased
with large amounts of clear to increase the magnification.
Naturalistic butterfly murrini float among roses and sunflowers.
Instead of creating layers of color, Ohkama makes beads that have
clearly defined interiors, where other worlds are suspended for
viewers to see. His recent work with borosilicate glass and bigger
torches includes pendants with a decidedly American twist.

▲ **Flower in the Water** | 1998–1999

Each: 2.5 x 2 x 2 cm
Lampworked; gold foil, murrini, Satake glass
Photo by Yoich Sueyoshi

" I am inspired by various
sources, such as photo
collections, kimono patterns,
and my hobby of movie-
watching. I strive to create
works that can inspire and
give dreams to people. As I
have learned the beauty of
the medium, I want people to
know the greatness of glass
beads and of lampwork. "

◀ **Hibiscus and Geometry** | 1999–2000

Left: 2.5 x 2 x 2 cm; Right: 2 x 2 x 2 cm
Lampworked, dot and scratch; Satake glass
Photo by Yoich Sueyoshi

▲ Dragonfly | 2004

2.5 x 2 x 2 cm

Lampworked; murrini, silver fume, Satake glass

Photo by artist

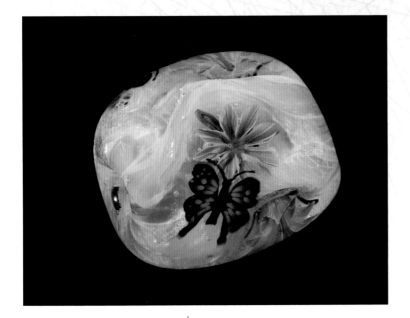

▲ **Butterfly on the Flower** | 2005

2.5 x 2 x 1.8 cm
Lampworked; silver fume, murrini, Satake glass
Photo by Yoich Sueyoshi

" Three or four years after my first glass work, I discovered contemporary glass beads and paperweights, and realized the diversity of lampwork. I became interested in the stereoscopic portraits seen in paperweights. My desire to create something like flowers or butterflies, with each part vividly blossoming or floating, drove me to produce such works. "

◀ **Sunflower** | 2005

2.5 x 2 x 2 cm
Lampworked; silver foil, murrini,
soda-lime glass
Photo by Yoich Sueyoshi

▲ **Geometry** | 2003

    2.5 x 2 x 2 cm
    Lampworked, scratched; Satake glass, gold foil
    Photo by Wakana Ogura

" My goal is to continue to create works with my own character, without regard to ancient patterns of glass beads. I never want to forget the fresh spirit I had at the beginning, the impulse for exploration. I want to broaden my horizons, to expand the possibilities of my work, not only in glass beads but also in lampwork. **"**

Geometry | 2006 ▶

    Left: 3.5 x 1.5 x 1.5 cm; right: 2 x 1.8 x 1.8 cm
    Lampworked; dot and scratch, gold foil,
    Satake glass
    Photo by Yoich Sueyoshi

▲ Boro Pendants, Dot and Rettcello, 2006

Left: 3 x 3 x 1.8 cm; right: 3 x 2.5 x 1.8 cm
Lampworked; gold fume; borosilicate glass

Photo by Yoich Sueyoshi

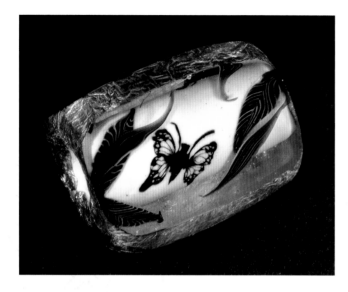

◀ **Butterfly and Leaf** │ 2005

3 x 2 x 2 cm
Lampworked; silver foil, murrini,
lace, Satake glass

Photo by Yoich Sueyoshi

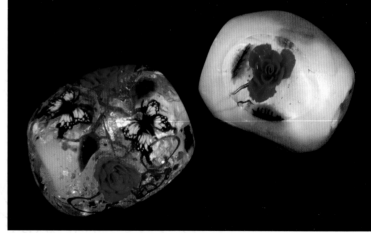

Rose & Butterfly and Rose │ 2003–2005 ▶

Left: 2.5 x 2 x 1.7 cm; right: 2.5 x 2 x 2 cm
Lampworked; isinglass, murrini; Satake glass

Photo by Yoich Sueyoshi

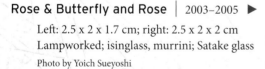

▲ **Butterfly and Flower** | 2006

3 x 2 x 2 cm
Lampworked; gold foil, murrini, Satake glass
Photo by Yoich Sueyoshi

AKIHIRO OHKAMA

Tom Holland

WHEN THE AMERICAN STUDIO glass bead making movement began in the late 1980s, Tom Holland was at the forefront. He and a handful of artists were the first serious bead makers in the United States. At the time, Holland was curious about how he could make beads himself, but he also wanted to know how beads had been made in the past.

Beads, of course, are mute messengers. They can't tell us how they were created. In order to learn the secrets of the past, Holland attempted to deconstruct the ancient Chinese Warring States bead in order to figure out how it might have been made. He used what he learned to reconstruct the bead on modern flameworking equipment. Holland also spent years unraveling the medieval Islamic folded bead—the Gordian Knot of bead making—and adapting it to the modern torch. His own beads are a melding of historical curiosity, exacting skill, and patience.

▲ **Golden Zhou** | 1999
3.1 x 2.4 x 2.4 cm
Lampworked; soft glass
Photo by Robert K. Lui/Ornament

▲ **Untitled** │ 1998

3.8 x 3 x 1 cm
Lampworked, coldworked; silver
foil, murrini; soda-lime glass

Photo by artist

▲ **Prefold** │ 1992

2 x 2 x 2 cm

Lampworked; multiple color cane

Photo by artist

▲ **Flaming Star** │ 2006

5 x 1.4 x 1.4 cm

Lampworked; murrini, soda-lime glass

Photo by Robert K. Lui/Ornament

▲ **Red Moorish Window** │ 2006

5.4 x 1.1 x 1.1 cm

Lampworked, marvered, crosshatched, masked, feathered; soda-lime glass

Photo by Robert K. Lui/Ornament

" For me, glass bead making is the ultimate experience in terms of intimate involvement with fire. Even though I can't touch the hot glass while I'm working with it, I delight in the kinetic dance of the temperature. "

▲ **Double Fold Can Can** | 2006

3.3 x 3.6 x 1.4 cm
Lampworked, double folding, furrowing

Photo by Robert K. Lui/Ornament

Bent Family Cane on Foil | 2003 ▶

5.4 x 1.6 x .9 cm
Lampworked; silver foil; murrini, coldworked;
soda-lime glass

Photo by Robert K. Lui/Ornament

▲ **Untitled** | 2004

4 x 3.4 x 1.2 cm
Lampworked, coldworked, cut; soda-lime glass, murrini
Photo by artist

▲ **Lapidary Rhondell** │ 2000

4.6 x 4.6 x 1.3 cm
Lampworked, coldworked; soda-lime glass, murrini

Photo by artist

" I love seeking out ancient glass bead-making techniques.
History shows us so many different ways to make beads,
that I feel like we're just getting started. "

▲ Bent Furrowed Zebra | 2002

5.2 x 1.8 x 1.8 cm
Lampworked, furrowing, bending; soda-lime glass
Photo by artist

" An old bead can teach you new tricks,
whether it's an ancient bead, or one you
made yourself a few years ago. "

▲ **Bead of Life and Life's Full Circle** | 2003

Bead: 5.4 x .9 x .9 cm; ring: 3.7 x 2.9 x .9 cm
Lampworked, crosshatching, bending; suspension bead

Photo by Robert K. Lui/Ornament

▲ **Double Fold Heart Pendant** | 2006

3 x 2.3 x 1.3 cm
Lampworked, doublefolding, furrowing,
twisted cane,

Photo by Robert K. Lui/Ornament

Karen Ovington

AROUND 1400 B.C., a cargo vessel sank near Uluburun, on the southern coast of Turkey. Thousands of glass beads were scattered on the seabed there. Karen Ovington's corroded and encrusted beads look like they could have been recovered from that wreck.

Using a variety of colored frits and powders, Ovington builds up surface textures on her beads that resemble corals, algae, and mineral deposits. The rough-hewn shapes of the beads make them look like the fragments of familiar objects. One bead resembles part of a bottle stopper, another some sort of handle. It is impossible to identify the pieces conclusively. In an unorthodox choice of materials, Ovington uses German hot glass color for her beads rather than the more common soft glass rods. German glass, which is used by glass blowers, offers a wider palette of frits and powders, as well as colors with high metal content that can add a metallic shine to a bead.

▲ **Untitled** | 2004

3 x 2 x 2 cm

Lampworked, heat and gravity shaped; enamels; soda-lime glass

Photo by Tom Van Eynde

" What drives me to create is the very substance we work with—molten glass. We are all alchemists working with gems of glass in different ways, watching how light dances on our glass. The work requires discipline and respect. "

◀ **Untitled** | 2000

5 x 2 x 2 cm
Lampworked; heat and gravity shaped;
etched; enamels, soda-lime glass

Photo by Tom Van Eynde

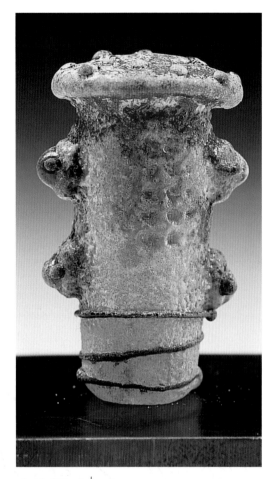

▲ **Untitled** | 2004

4 x 2.5 x 1.5 cm
Lampworked, heat and gravity shaped, etched;
enamels, stringers, soda-lime glass

Photo by Tom Van Eynde

▲ **Untitled** | 2002

5 x 2 x 3 cm
Lampworked, heat and gravity shaped, etched;
enamels, frits, stringers, soda-lime glass

Photo by Robert Liu

▼ **Untitled** | 1996

3 x 4 x 1 cm
Lampworked, heat and gravity shaped; glass frits,
enamels, stringers, soda-lime glass

Photo by Tom Van Eynde

◀ **Untitled** | 1999

5 x 3 x 2 cm
Lampworked, heat and gravity shaped, etched;
enamels, soda-lime glass

Photo by Tom Van Eynde

" My work is spontaneous. I feel free when I'm at the torch. I don't gravitate to the technical aspects of making beads as some artists do. As a result, my beads may not be perfectly round, but they will have color and texture. I let the glass dictate to me. "

◀ **Untitled** | 2002

6 x 4 x 2 cm
Lampworked, heat and gravity shaped, etched; enamels, stringers, soda-lime glass

Photo by Tom Van Eynde

" The colors and textures in glass create a restless curiosity in me. I am never content to simply repeat myself. I try to stay away from conformity. I find it important to seek direction from within rather than from the replication of other artists' work. "

◀ **Untitled** | 2003

5 x 2 x 1 cm
Lampworked, heat and gravity shaped,
etched; enamels, soda-lime glass
Photo by Tom Van Eynde

KAREN OVINGTON

▲ **Untitled** │ 1996

3.5 x 3.5 x 1 cm
Lampworked, heat and gravity shaped, etched;
enamels, stringers, soda-lime glass

Photo by Tom Van Eynde

▲ **Untitled** | 2003

6 x 3 x 1 cm
Lampworked, heat and gravity shaped, etched; enamels, soda-lime glass

Photo by Tom Van Eynde

PETERS

Sharon Peters

MAKE NO MISTAKE ABOUT IT—Sharon Peters' beads
are not your normal, run-of-the-mill beads. They jump up
and down. They yell and scream. They talk back, and they
sometimes use bad words. They can't and won't be ignored.
The jokes, puns, and general foolishness that inspire Peters
to make these beads can sometimes obscure the skill and
innovation that she uses to make them.

Doing sculptural work with glass beads can be very
challenging, due to the small scale. While working on
one part of a bead, other sections can crack or melt flat.
The design has to be economical, with just enough detail
to make the desired point or, in this case, pun. Despite
their diminutive scale, Peters' beads always succeed in
communicating their meaning. Her beads are unusual, but
they are good beads. As she might say herself, "No good bead
should go unpunished."

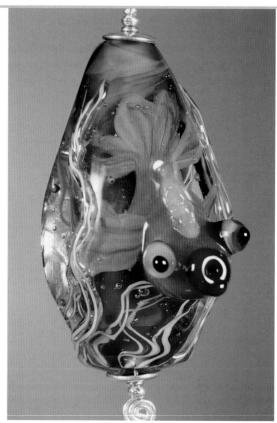

▲ **Carpe Diem** | 1999

5 x 2.8 x 3.5 cm
Lampworked, heat and gravity shaped, multi-layer
casing, sculpted; soda-lime glass

Photo by Jim Trenkle

▲ **Chinese New Year Dragon** | 2005

10.5 x 5.5 x 4.5 cm

Lampworked, heat and gravity shaped, sculpted; soda-lime glass

Photo by Jim Trenkle

▲ **How can you tell it's winter? Frogsicle!!** | 2003

6 x 6 x 4 cm

Lampworked; heat and gravity shaped, sculpted; multi-beads on silver wire, soda-lime glass

Photo by Jim Trenkle

▲ **Poultry in Motion** | 2002

7 x 3 x 3 cm

Lampworked, heat and gravity shaped, sculpted, tea stained; metallic flex wire, silver findings, seed beads, soda-lime glass

Photo by Jim Trenkle

" Playing with fire and dripping hot glass is like messing with liquid light. It's absolutely fascinating and involving, and—since pieces can be created in hours instead of days—it offers instant gratification, too. Lots of playtime at the torch generates lots of new ideas, and eventually a personal style. "

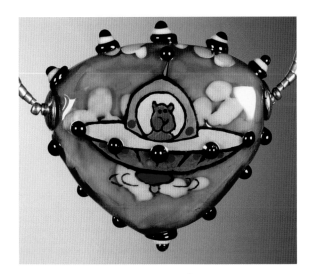

▲ **Take Me to Your Beader** | 2004

5.5 x 5 x 1 cm
Lampworked, heat and gravity shaped; vitreous enamel paint, soda-lime glass

Photo by Jim Trenkle

▲ **New Orc, New Orc . . .** | 2000

4.5 x 4 x 2 cm
Lampworked; heat and gravity shaped, sculpted, tea stained; soda-lime glass

Photo by Jim Trenkle

SHARON PETERS

▲ Yipes, Stripes! | 2004

5 x 4 x 2 cm
Lampworked, heat and gravity shaped,
sculpted, painted, soda-lime glass

Photo by Jim Trenkle

▼ Urine Trouble | 2006

4 x 3 x 2.5 cm
Lampworked, heat and gravity shaped,
sculpted; steel, soda-lime glass

Photo by Jim Trenkle

SHARON PETERS

" I do representational pieces—concepts made into 3-D images. Every design has an idea, a name, and a story. I do a fast doodle, crank up the kiln, light the torch and give it a try. Then I'll be lost for weeks experimenting with form, modifying and morphing designs, and tinkering with techniques. "

▲ Beanie Kids | 1998

Boy: 6 x 3.5 x 2.5 cm; girl: 6 x 2.5 x 1.5 cm
Lampworked, heat and gravity shaped, sculpted; multi-bead silver wire, soda-lime glass

Photo by Jim Trenkle

▲ Cheaper by the Galleon | 2006

7 x 7 x 3 cm
Lampworked, heat and gravity shaped, sculpted, tea stained; steel, silver foil, soda-lime glass

Photo by Jim Trenkle

SHARON PETERS

▲ **Ghouls Just Wanna Have Fun** | 2003

9.5 x 6 x 5 cm
Lampworked, heat and gravity shaped, sculpted;
multi-bead, silver wire, soda-lime glass

Photo by Jim Trenkle

" Creating is a personal thing. The best work always comes out of something inside you, that's part of you. And if the thing you make speaks to others, you've accomplished something. What you 'say' and what they 'hear' may not be the same, but if your work makes somebody feel something, then you're on your way to being an artist. "

▲ **Goof Dragon** | 2005

4.5 x 6.5 x 6.5 cm
Lampworked, heat and gravity shaped,
sculpted, tea-stained; soda-lime glass

Photo by Jim Trenkle

Yoshiko Shiiba

THE MURRINI FLOWERS AND LEAVES on Yoshiko Shiiba's beads pile up in drifts as if blown there by a soft breeze. There is a haiku-like simplicity and directness about her work. With more than twenty-five years experience as a bead maker, Shiiba has the knowledge and skill to create beads that would rival those of any maker in color and complexity. Yet her beads are restrained. They are economical and sublime.

Many bead makers say that the process is a meditative one, that the actual making of a bead is more important than the finished product. Shiiba's bead-making meditations end with "There. Enough."

◀ **Blue Hana Ranbu** | 2006
2 x 1.5 to 2.5 x 2 cm
Lampworked; soft glass
Photo by Takayuki Mastuzawa

▲ Renka │ 2003

1.5 x 1.5 to 2.5 x 1.5 cm
Lampworked; soft glass

Photo by artist

▲ **Genroku Dama** | 2002

    2 x 1.5 to 3 x 2 cm
    Lampworked; soft glass
    Photo by artist

▲ **Cherry Blossom and Water Stream** | 2003

    1.5 x 1.5 to 2.5 x 1.5 cm
    Lampworked; soft glass
    Photo by artist

▲ **Genroku-dama (for Obi-dome)** | 1998

4 x 1.5 cm
Lampworked; soft glass

Photo by artist

" I think I was born to love glass
in general as a medium—not only
lampworking, but also furnace blowing,
casting, fusing, and pâte de verre. "

▲ **Red Genroku Dama** | 1998

2 x 1.5 cm
Lampworked; soft glass
Photo by artist

▲ **Yuzen** | 1996

2 x 1.5 cm
Lampworked; soft glass
Photo by artist

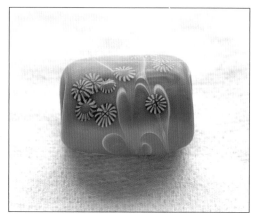

▲ **Chrysanthemum and Stream (for Obi-dome)** | 2003

3 x 2.5 cm
Lampworked; soft glass
Photo by artist

▲ **Hana Ranbu** | 2006

2.5 x 2 cm
Lampworked; soft glass
Photo by Takayuki Mastuzawa

▲ **Hana-zukushi** | 2000

Left: 3 x 2.5 cm
Right: 1.5 x 1.5 cm
Lampworked; soft glass
Photo by artist

▲ **Autumn Leaves** | 2006

2.5 x 1.5 to 4 x 1.5 cm
Lampworked; soft glass

Photo by Takayuki Mastuzawa

" Seeing ancient tombodama at the Shosoin

Temple in Nara, Japan, seemed like destiny.

I was inspired by those beautiful beads.

They led me to bead making. "

▲ Chigusa (Kohshi-dama) | 2006

4 x 1.5 cm
Lampworked; soft glass
Photo by Takayuki Mastuzawa

" When I begin work, I come up with the images of my design, and then I apply those images to actual forms. That process, not just the result, is what I cherish the most about this work. I believe that this is what has inspired me and made me work on glass for so many years. "

YOSHIKO SHIIBA

Jim Smircich

EVERYONE KNOWS THAT HEAT is essential to the process of making glass beads, yet few bead makers take heat as seriously as Jim Smircich. Glass is a poor conductor of heat—it heats slowly and cools slowly. But the way that glass retains heat, combined with rotation and gravity, allows Smircich to form the overall shapes of his beads, as well as some of his surface patterns, without using any tools at all.

Some colors and types of glass react to each other in unexpected ways. Smircich uses the physical properties of glass itself to shape his beads. He doesn't resort to marvering. With adroit use of the flame, Smircich makes his colors to dissolve into each other, creating intricate webs of contrasting shades as he works.

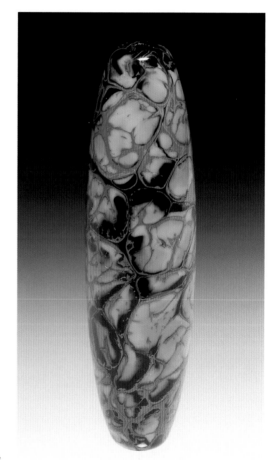

Turquoise in Matrix | 2002 ▶
1.3 x 5 cm
Lampworked, tumbled; soda-lime glass
Photo by Joanie Beldin

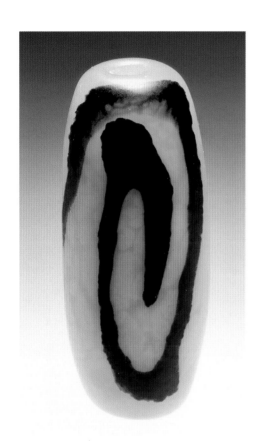

▲ **Tumbled Petroglyph** │ 1995

1.3 x 3.1 cm
Lampworked; tumbled; soda-lime glass

Photo by Joanie Beldin

▲ **Apple Core** │ 1993

2 x 4.8 cm
Lampworked; soda-lime glass

Photo by Joanie Beldin

" When I helped found the International
Society of Glass Beadmakers, it seemed
that it was time to bring bead making
forward into the realm of the fine arts.
I believe that the North American bead
movement has reached that plateau.
Not only are we offering beads as fine
art—we are also providing our expertise
as teachers to the world. "

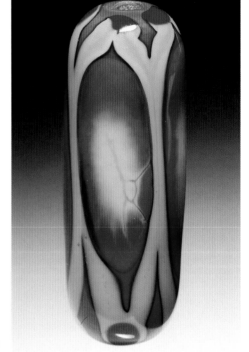

Caged Coral | 1996 ▶

1.2 x 3.4 cm
Lampworked; soda-lime glass
Photo by Joanie Beldin

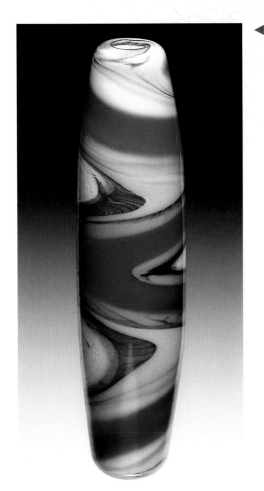

◀ **Carnival Wave** | 1996

1.1 x 4.5 cm
Lampworked, gravity pro-
duced; soda-lime glass

Photo by Joanie Beldin

▲ **Untitled** | 2006

Left: 1.5 x 2.2 cm; right: 1.3 x 2 cm
Lampworked; tumbled; soda-lime glass

Photo by Joanie Beldin

JIM SMIRCICH

▲ **Black and White Knuckle Bone** │ 1992

1.4 x 3.6 cm
Lampworked; soda-lime glass

Photo by Joanie Beldin

" To master the art of bead making, you must
find the center of a moving mass of hot glass
and bring it to a solid state with your creative
passion shining forth for all to see. "

▼ **Leopard Stripes/Tiger Spots** | 2006

1.6 x 4.2 cm
Lampworked; tumbled; soda-lime glass
Photo by Joanie Beldin

▲ **Weasel Eye** | 1994

1.3 x 4.7 cm
Lampworked; soda-lime glass
Photo by Joanie Beldin

JIM SMIRCICH

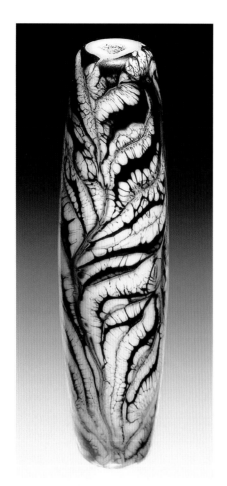

▲ **Black Lace** | 2000

1.2 x 4.4 cm
Lampworked, heat and gravity shaped,
tumbled; soda-lime glass

Photo by Joanie Beldin

▼ **Silver Metal Tracery** | 2003

1.6 x 4 cm
Lampworked, heat and gravity
shaped; soda-lime glass, silver fume

Photo by Joanie Beldin

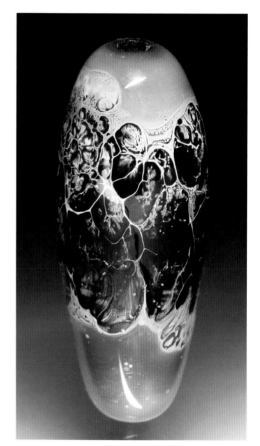

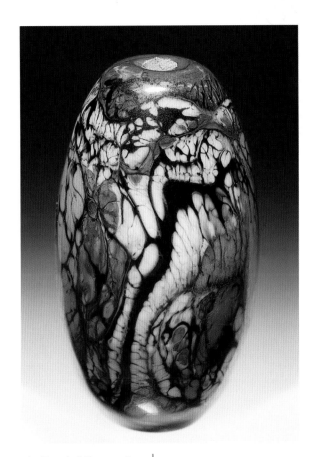

▲ **Fractal Geometry** | 2005

1.9 x 3.5 cm
Lampworked, heat and gravity shaped, tumbled;
block glass, ivory and grey soda-lime glass

Photo by Joanie Beldin

" When I make a worthy bead for
the first time, I make twenty
more. This allows me to refine and
master my creative moments. "

Kate Fowle Meleney

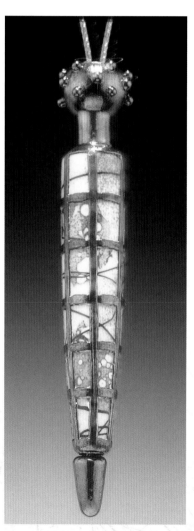

SOME OF KATE FOWLE MELENEY'S BEADS are tidy and sensible, and some are not. Some pieces look like shells or barnacle-laden rocks that could have come right off the beach. Her Paleolithic goddess and cave painting beads are a nod to the object makers of our remote past. These beads are well-made and well-behaved. Then there are the others.

Meleney makes glass forms inspired by nature and encloses them in an electroformed skin. Electroforming is the building up of a metal coating on the surface of objects that do not conduct electricity. Using a copper paint, Meleney creates lines and grids on lampworked beads. The beads are then hung in a metal, ion-rich solution. With very low-voltage electricity, layer after layer of metal is slowly deposited on the copper paint. Some of these electroformed beads resemble pods that have washed up on an alien shore. Others, with a grid of metal straps, seem intent on keeping that sensible, well-behaved glass bead inside from escaping.

◀ **Anthropomorph** │ 2003
8 x 1.5 x 1.5 cm
Lampworked, sculpted, electroformed;
enamels, copper leaf, soda-lime glass
Photo by Jerry Anthony

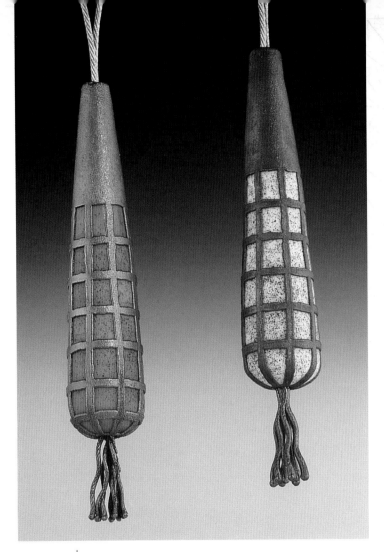

" I came to this medium with
a background in jewelry and
creating wearable art is my final
aim when I sit down to a torch. "

▲ Yurts | 2003

8.5 x 2 x 2 cm
Lampworked, sculpted, etched, electroformed;
enamel, soda-lime glass

Photo by Jerry Anthony

▲ **Petroglyph Tabular** | 1996

3 x 4.5 x 1.5 cm
Lampworked, heat and paddle shaped; copper and
silver leaf, overglazes, soda-lime glass

Photo by Jerry Anthony

▲ **Mudcloth Bead** | 2000

6.5 x 2 x 2 cm
Lampworked, sculpted, silver fumed, electroformed; overglazes, soda-lime glass

Photo by Jerry Anthony

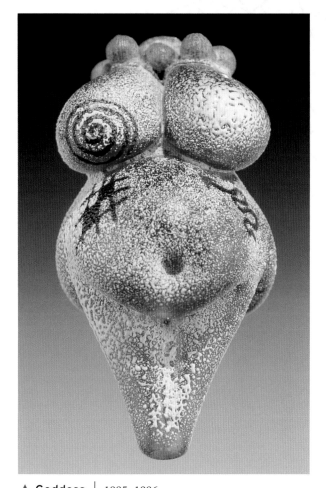

▲ Goddess | 1995–1996

5 x 2.5 x 2.5 cm
Lampworked, sculpted, etched,
electroformed; enamels, overglazes,
soda-lime glass

Photo by Jerry Anthony

" I frequently ponder how long beads have been an important adornment—so much longer than history can relate—and I love to think that I am continuing with that tradition when I work at the torch. "

MELENEY

" My interest is in creating beads that can stand alone as sculpture, with a subtle reference to familiar shapes from nature. Ancient glass, ethnic art, and textiles are additional pattern and texture sources for me. "

◀ Aegean Urn | 1996

7 x 2 x 2 cm
Lampworked, sculpted, etched; gold leaf, enamels, millefiori, soda-lime glass
Photo by Jerry Anthony

" In the flora and fauna of our world, there is
a fascinating tension between symmetry and
irregularity, which I try to reflect in my work. "

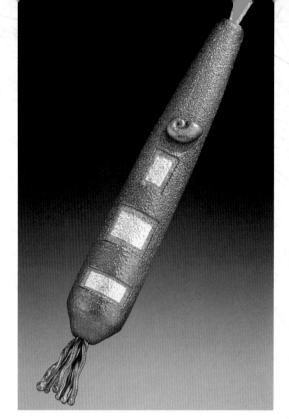

▲ **Neptune's Collage** | 2004
8.5 x 2 x 2 cm
Lampworked, sculpted, electroformed;
enamels and gold foil, soda-lime glass
Photo by Jerry Anthony

▲ **Seashells** | 1994
Largest: 3.2 x 2 x 2 cm
Lampworked, sculpted, masked and etched;
soda-lime glass, millefiori
Photo by Bronwen Sexton

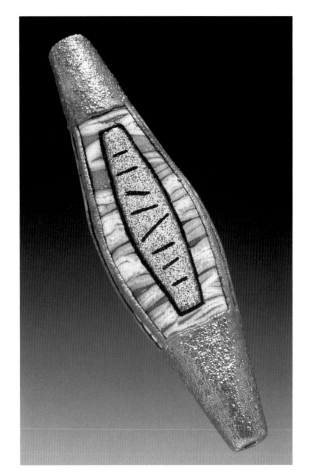

▼ Red Sea Pod | 2004

9.5 x 1.8 x 1.8 cm
Lampworked, sculpted, electroformed;
soda-lime glass
Photo by Jerry Anthony

▲ Open Pod | 2003

7 x 3 x 1.5 cm
Lampworked, sculpted, silver fumed, electroformed;
enamels and overglazes, soda-lime glass
Photo by Jerry Anthony

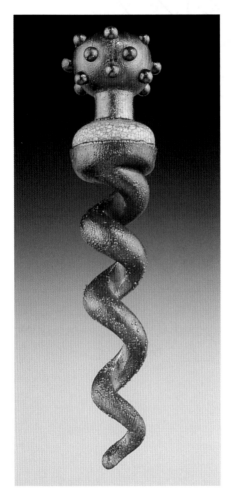

▲ **Spiral** | 2003

8 x 1.5 x 1.5 cm
Lampworked, sculpted, etched, silver
fumed, electroformed; soda-lime glass
Photo by Jerry Anthony

▼ **Green Hydra** | 2004

8 x 2.2 x 2.2 cm
Lampworked, sculpted, etched; electroformed;
silver and copper leaf, soda-lime glass
Photo by Jerry Anthony

Norikazu Kogure

TONBO-DAMA—A DRAGONFLY'S EYE—is the Japanese term for glass bead. Norikazu Kogure literally wrote the book on the subject in 2006 with his volume *Tonbo-dama (Japanese Glass Beads)*. A consummate technician and enthusiastic advocate of glass bead making, Kogure is a master of the art. It seems there is nothing that he cannot do. Detailed mosaic canes, frilly lace canes, and layered colors appear again and again in his beads.

Kogure brings a unique nuance to each of his designs. Some of his beads feature white ribbon canes that become rainbow canes, with the colors gradually blending through the length of the bead as the cane coils around it. In other pieces, white lace canes float above core beads that run the full spectrum of colors. While Kogure's work is clearly grounded in the Japanese bead-making tradition, his beads do not come from someone else's recipe book. They reflect his original vision and singular skill.

▲ **Gold-Band Bead** | 2006
6 x 1.5 x 1.5 cm
Lampworked; dichroic glass, soda-lime glass
Photo by artist

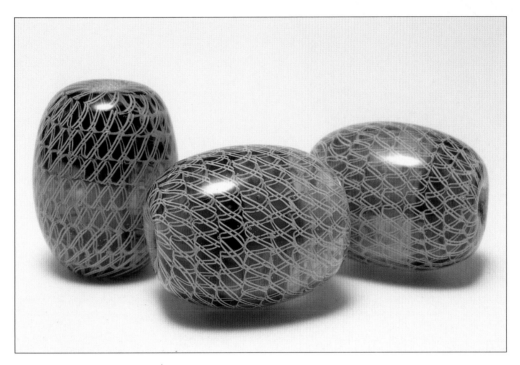

▲ Twisted Cane Beads | 2004

2.5 x 2.2 x 2.2 cm
Lampworked; handmade twisted cane, Satake
glass

Photo by artist

◄ **Imagine BOTAN** │ 2006

2.5 x 2.2 x 2.2 cm
Lampworked; handmade murrini, handmade
twisted cane, Satake glass

Photo by artist

KIKU in Water │ 2006 ▶

2.5 x 2.2 x 2.2 cm
Lampworked; handmade murrini,
silver leaf, Satake glass

Photo by artist

" My education in art began with craft design. Believe it or not, the subject I chose was plastic. Since I was charmed by the transparent material, the progression from plastic to glass was natural for me. I am interested in areas of art that require elaborate and delicate work, similar to the traditional Japanese fine arts. Lampworking is like this. "

▲ HANA-ZUKUSHI Beads | 2006
2.5 x 2.3 x 2.3 cm
Lampworked; handmade murrini, silver leaf, Satake glass
Photo by artist

SAKURA in Midnight | 2005 ▶

2.2 x 2 x 2 cm
Lampworked; handmade murrini,
silver leaf, Satake glass

Photo by artist

▼ **SAKURA with Water** | 2006

2.5 x 2.2 x 2.2 cm
Lampworked; handmade murrini,
silver leaf, Satake glass

Photo by artist

▲ **Imagine SAKURA** | 2006

2.5 x 2.2 x 2.2 cm
Lampworked; handmade murrini, handmade twisted cane, Satake glass

Photo by artist

▼ Imagine SAKURA | 2006

2.5 x 2.2 x 2.2 cm
Lampworked; handmade murrini,
handmade twisted cane, gold leaf,
Satake glass

Photo by artist

" I grew up immersed in the long
history of Japan and its artistic
cultures. Both have influenced me.
So has Japan's natural beauty, in
each of the four seasons. There is
a Japanese word, *ten-shoku*, which
can be translated as "God-given
job." Being a glass artist is the *ten-
shoku* for me. **"**

SAKURA | 2006 ▶

2.5 x 2.2 x 2.2 cm
Lampworked; handmade murrini,
gold leaf, Satake glass

Photo by artist

▲ **Rainbow Twisted Cane Bead** | 2006

2.5 x 2.2 x 2.2 cm
Lampworked; handmade twisted cane, Satake glass

Photo by artist

▲ TAKARA-ZUKUSHI | 2004

3 x 2.5 x 2.5 cm
Lampworked; handmade murrini, gold leaf,
Satake glass

Photo by artist

" As a student, my exposure
to beautiful, highly technical
mosaics and core glasses from
ancient Rome awakened my
interest in glass. I was taught
by Kisao Iburi and Iwao
Matsushima. Their teachings
and masterpieces inspired me
and fixed my future direction in
glass art. "

KOGURE

Gail Crosman Moore

▲ **Spiral** | 2004

8 x 2.5 cm
Lampworked, heat, gravity, and marver
formed; borosilicate glass

Photo by Charley Freiberg

DIATOMS AND FLAGELLATES, seeds and pods, plants and animals—all of these can be found in the work of Gail Crosman Moore. She creates her forms from borosilicate glass, a material that is more shock-resistant than typical soft glass. The strength of borosilicate glass gives Moore the freedom to explore shapes that would be unwearable if made from a material that was less sturdy.

Color in borosilicate glass is an inconsistent thing. Temperature and time in both the torch and the annealing kiln affect the final color of the glass. Moore uses this color serendipity to her advantage. A set of her beads presents a variety of shades of color "ripeness." Moore also repeats simple flameworking techniques again and again in her work. Lines become spirals, which evolve into vine motifs. Dots are stretched and flattened into sepals and petals. Moore's jewelry pieces also feature hand-felted wool, which she uses for the stems and leaves of her glass blossoms.

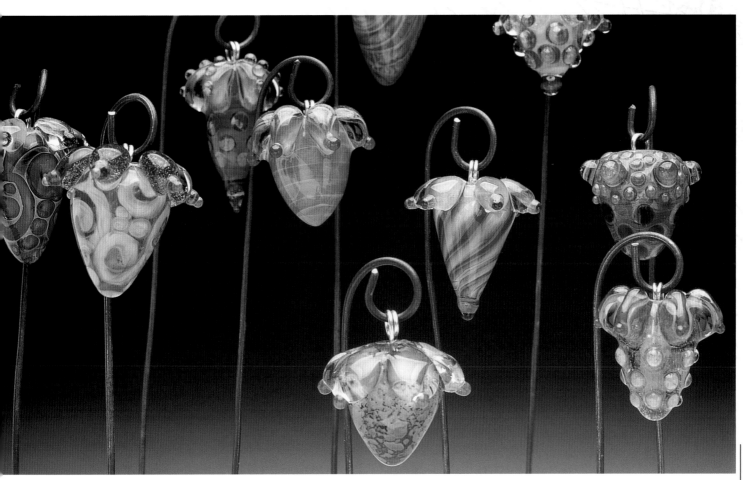

▲ **Menagerie of Pendants** | 2000

    2 x 3 cm
    Lampworked, heat, gravity, and marver
    formed; borosilicate glass

    Photo by Charley Freiberg

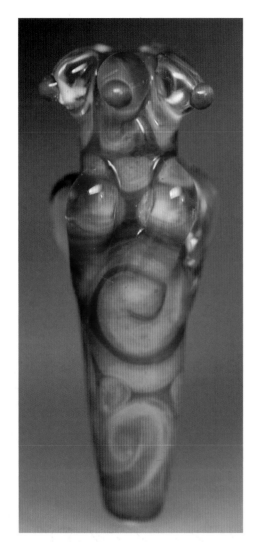

"My vision as an artist
is to strive to continue
to grow, change, and
experiment, using what
has come before as
information towards the
next step. This life is a
balancing act between
my time, energy, and
resources. The nature
of my work calls for a
commitment to detail that
I find ever challenging."

▲ Fire | 2004
    8 x 2.2 cm
    Lampworked, heat, gravity, and
    marver formed; clear lobes,
    borosilicate glass
    Photo by artist

▲ Green Amphora | 2004
    7 x 2.5 cm
    Lampworked, heat, gravity, and
    marver formed; borosilicate glass
    Photo by artist

▲ **Silver Blues** | 1997

Longest: 8 cm; most: 3 to 3.5 cm
Lampworked, heat and gravity shaped,
marvered; silver leaf, borosilicate glass

Photo by artist

▲ **Spiral Bound** | 2004

5 x 4.3 cm
Lampworked, gold fumed; borosilicate glass

Photo by artist

" Horticulture and growing up by the sea have given me a wealth of inspiration, as well as a vocabulary of form, color, and texture that I rely on in my art making. Life in all of its bounty continues to provide me with a wealth of materials to manipulate. I strive to try them all. "

▲ Vertebrae | 1997

Each: 2 x 4 cm
Lampworked, heat and gravity shaped, acid etched; soda-lime glass

Photo by artist

▲ Lone Acorn | 2006

3 x 1.5 cm
Lampworked, heat, gravity, and marver formed, fired, patinaed; metal clay

Photo by Charley Freiberg

Ocean Green | 2006 ▶

7 x 3 cm
Lampworked, heat, gravity, and marver
formed, sandblasted; borosilicate glass

Photo by Charley Freiberg

◀ **Blasted Pair** | 2006

4 x 2.6 cm
Lampworked, heat, gravity, and
marver formed, mashed, pulled,
sandblasted

Photo by Charley Freiberg

" The organic forms that I create are coming closer to succinctly saying what I've only recently been able to identify and articulate. The notion of emergence or an inner life force through allusions to pods, eggs, and seeds, which symbolize life and hope, continues to permeate my work. "

▲ **Wired and Spiral** | 2005

60 x 2.5 cm
Lampworked, heat, gravity, and marver
formed, mashed and pulled; borosilicate
glass, crocheted rope

Photo by artist

▲ **Purple Flower** | 2003

85 x 13 cm
Lampworked, heat, gravity, and marver formed; borosilicate glass;
hand-felted marino fleece

Photo by Charley Freiberg

Mary Mullaney and Ralph Mossman

▲ **Blue Malachite Chevrons** | 1999

2.5 x 3 cm
Furnace worked, blown and drawn; coldworked,
cut, hand-ground, tumbler polished; soda-lime glass
Photo by Mary Mullaney

CHEVRON BEADS WERE first made in Venetian glass factories in the late fifteenth century. Today, these classic beads are made on the end of a blowpipe, then dipped into color, and pressed into star molds. Mary Mullaney and Ralph Mossman, partners in Heron Glass, make chevron beads, but they have dispensed with the traditional hot pots of molten color. Their canes are made of bars of color wrapped around a small bubble of glass on the end of a blowpipe.

Mullaney and Mossman sometimes add multiple layers of color rods with a casing of molten clear between each layer. They also substitute complex and colorful canes for the solid color rods. After the bubble is pulled into a long tube and cut into pieces, each piece is hand-ground into a chevron bead. With this updated version of an old technique, Mullaney and Mossman create chevrons that feature intricate patterns, sharp detail, and rich color.

▲ **Murrini Cane Bead** | 1994

3 x 3 x 3 cm
Furnace worked, blown and drawn, coldworked, cut,
hand-ground, tumbler polished; soda-lime glass

Photo by Mary Mullaney

" Beads are intriguing because
of their extensive history—they
inevitably gain from the many
different hands they pass
through. They were probably
the first form of art. Over
time, beads can become very
precious and powerful objects.
I like the idea of my work being
transformed in a similar way. "

Amber Cane Chevron | 1996 ▶

2 x 2 x 2 cm
Furnace worked, blown and drawn,
coldworked, cut, hand-ground, tumbler polished; soda-lime glass

Photo by Mary Mullaney

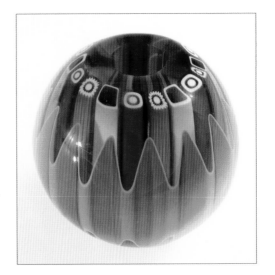

▲ **Rainbow and Rasta Chevrons** | 2005

Largest: 2.5 x 4 cm
Furnace worked, blown and drawn, coldworked, cut, hand-
ground, tumbler polished; soda-lime glass

Photo by Mary Mullaney

Pine Green Chevrons | 1999 ▶

2.5 x 4 cm
Furnace worked, blown and drawn,
coldworked, cut, hand-ground, tumbler
polished; soda-lime glass

Photo by Mary Mullaney

◀ **Purple, Red, and Orange Chevron** | 2001

2 x 5 cm
Furnace worked, blown and drawn, coldworked, cut,
hand-ground, tumbler polished; soda-lime glass

Photo by Mary Mullaney

▲ **Brown and Olive Chevron** | 2002

Talest: 2.5 x 5 cm
Furnace worked, blown and drawn, coldworked, cut, hand-ground, tumbler polished;
soda-lime glass
Photo by Mary Mullaney

▲ **Chameleon Chevrons** | 2006

Tallest: 2 x 3 cm
Furnace worked, blown and drawn, coldworked,
cut, hand-ground, tumbler polished; soda-lime
glass
Photo by Mary Mullaney

" We challenge ourselves by utilizing difficult Italian blowing techniques, so that these techniques aren't lost or ignored. Our artistic goal is to create beads that evoke wonder and incredulity from complexity, detail, and exquisite color combinations. "

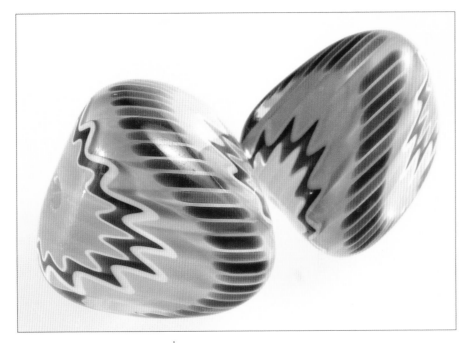

▲ Tetrahedral Chevrons | 1992

2 x 2.5 x 2 cm
Furnace worked, blown and drawn, coldworked, cut, hand-ground, tumbler polished; soda-lime glass
Photo by Mary Mullaney

▲ **Green and Purple Bicone Chevron** | 2001

2 x 3 cm
Furnace worked, blown and drawn, coldworked, cut, hand-ground, tumbler polished; soda-lime glass

Photo by Mary Mullaney

" Glass is especially interesting to me because of its lasting qualities. Often, when looking at ancient glass, I wonder and fantasize about the lives of historic craftspeople. This is a source of inspiration for me and a connection to the past. "

▲ **Gray Cane Chevrons** | 1995

2.5 x 3 cm
Furnace worked, blown and drawn, cold-worked, cut, hand-ground, tumbler polished; soda-lime glass

Photo by Mary Mullaney

▲ **Peach Chevron and Lime Chevron** | 2006

Left: 2.5 x 3 cm; right: 2 x 4 cm
Furnace worked, blown and drawn, coldworked, cut, hand-
ground, tumbler polished; soda-lime glass

Photo by Mary Mullaney

Kristen Frantzen Orr

LOOKING AT THE WORK of Kristen Frantzen Orr, it comes as no surprise that she has an enduring interest in watercolor and calligraphy. Her floral blossoms are characterized by the soft hues seen in watercolor paintings. Vines and stems wind like the extended serifs of calligraphy through her beads.

Orr employs round, flattened, striped, or ribbed canes as if they were the brushes used in watercolor and calligraphy. The result is like writing with flowers. A raised filigree of blossoms and stems wraps each of her beads. Neither the blossoms nor the stems are portrayed as identifiable plants. Everything is merely suggested. Orr's floral beads have a Belle Époque sensibility characterized by dreamy colors and twining lines. For the viewer, the effect provides a momentary escape from the real world.

◀ **Vermillion Promise** │ 2002

4.8 x 1.7 x 1.7 cm
Lampworked, heat and gravity shaped,
etched, marvered; striped cane, soda-lime
glass
Photo by David Orr

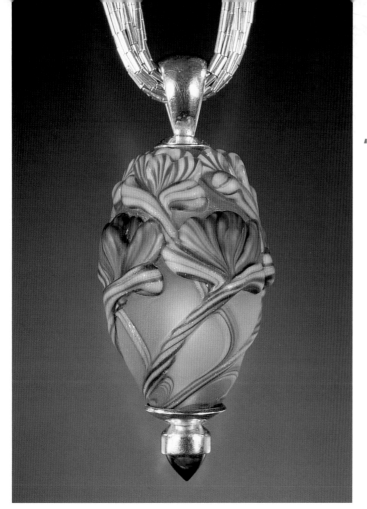

" Light fascinates me. The nature of glass provides a means for capturing light and reflecting it. When exploring color and texture, contrast becomes important. I like to etch portions of a bead and leave the rest of the surface shiny. I'm enchanted by the magic of the flame, and I like the immediacy of the work, the instant gratification. "

▲ **Amanda's Bouquet** | 2004

3.3 x 2 x 1.4 cm
Lampworked, heat and gravity shaped, etched, marvered; striped cane; soda-lime glass
Photo by David Orr

▲ **Encased Floral Globe Beads** | 1995

2.3 x 2.3 x 2.3 cm
Lampworked, heat and gravity shaped, marvered; soda-lime glass
Photo by Jeff Scovil

MASTERS: GLASS BEADS

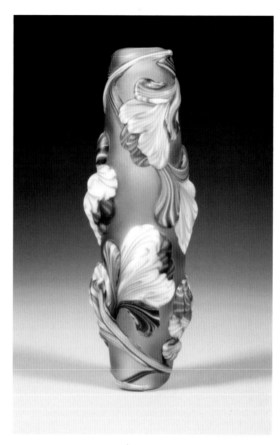

▲ **Luminescent** | 2001

    5 x 1.5 x 1.5 cm

    Lampworked, heat and gravity shaped, etched, marvered; striped cane; soda-lime glass

    Photo by David Orr

▲ **Autumn Honey** | 2006

    5 x 1.7 x 1.7 cm

    Lampworked, heat and gravity shaped, marvered, etched; striped cane; soda-lime glass

    Photo by David Orr

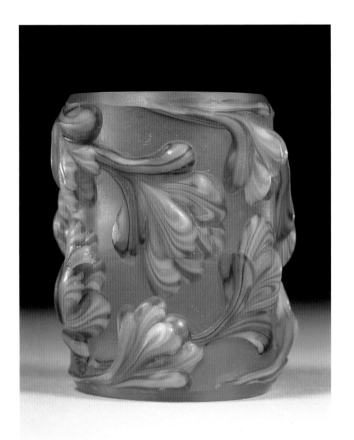

" In my own mind, color is probably the most important aspect of my work. Usually in my beads, colors are layered or overlapped in some way to create a play of hues. Placing the right colors next to each other really makes them sing! "

▲ **Marmalade** | 2001

2.8 x 2.4 x 2.4 cm
Lampworked, heat and gravity shaped, etched, marvered; striped cane; soda-lime glass

Photo by David Orr

▲ **Modern Victorian** | 2006

4.2 x 3.9 x 1.5 cm
Lampworked, flattened and shaped, etched;
frit; striped cane; soda-lime glass

Photo by David Orr

▼ **Mountain Twilight** | 2002

3.9 x 3.7 x 1.6 cm
Lampworked, flattened and shaped, etched;
enamels and copper leaf; striped cane; soda-
lime glass

Photo by David Orr

▲ **Celebration** | 2003

5 x 1.6 x 1.6 cm
Lampworked, heat and gravity shaped, etched, marvered; goldstone stringer; striped cane; soda-lime glass

Photo by David Orr

▲ **Opalescent Coral Floral** | 2005

6 x 1.6 x 1.6 cm
Lampworked, heat and gravity shaped, etched, marvered; striped cane; soda-lime glass

Photo by David Orr

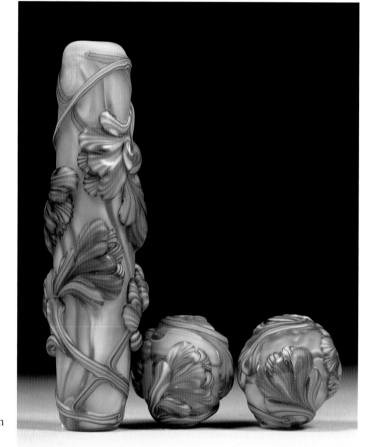

Can't Find Pearls in the Desert | 2002 ▶

Long: 5 x 1.5 x 1.5 cm; round: 1.5 x 1.5 x 1.5 cm
Lampworked, heat and gravity shaped, etched,
marvered; striped cane; soda-lime glass

Photo by David Orr

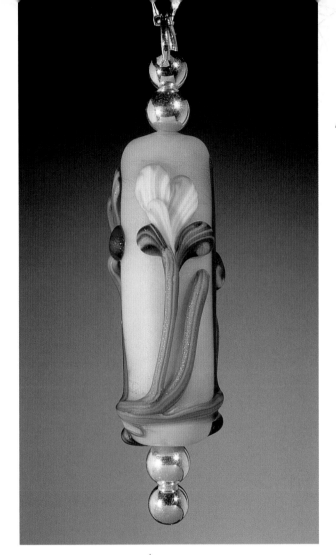

▲ Iris on Nile Green | 1997

3.2 x 1.2 x 1.2 cm
Lampworked, heat and gravity shaped, etched,
marvered; striped cane; soda-lime glass

Photo by Jeff Scovil

" My history with watercolors and calligraphy has directed my path. I discovered I could create something similar to gradient brush strokes by encasing opaque glass with dark transparent colors. With calligraphic marks, it's possible to convey gesture and movement in a minimum number of strokes. This is useful when working on a surface as small as a glass bead. "

Toshimasa Masui

A DOT ON A WHITE BEAD is the starting point for many of Toshimasa Masui's creations. From a technical standpoint, Masui's work is reduced to the absolute minimum. He uses a single dot, overlapping dots, and raking to create the patterns on his compact, white barrel beads. There are no mosaic sections, twisted canes, or frits and powders involved in his bead making process.

Masui employs the simple dot to create wonderfully complex patterns. The curved stems of his vines are formed from overlapping dots. The vine leaves are concentric dots elongated with the end of a fine stringer of glass. Masui teases flower petals, leaves, twigs, stars, rectangles out of dots. What could be more simple? Perhaps only an all-white bead.

◀ **Mission** | 2001
4.5 x 3.2 cm
Lampworked; dots, Satake glass
Photo by artist

▲ **Untitled** | 2004

3.5 x 2.8 cm
Lampworked, raked, dots, threaded
stringer; Satake glass

Photo by artist

▲ **Chinese Phoenix** | 1999

3 x 2.7 cm
Lampworked, raked; dots, Satake glass
Photos by artist

" I became interested in bead making many years ago, when I saw Japanese glass beads called *tombo-dama*. I felt these small beads of glass were so beautiful and wondered how they could contain so many fine colored patterns. There is no limit in *tombo-dama* to artistic expression and possibility. "

▲ Tang Grass | 1999

4.5 x 4.1 cm

Lampworked; dots, Satake glass

Photo by artist

▲ Grape Tang Grass | 1999

4.5 x 3.9 cm

Lampworked; raked; dots, Satake glass

Photo by artist

▲ **MANDARA** | 2000

4.5 x 3.5 cm
Lampworked, raked; dots, Satake glass
Photo by artist

▲ **Untitled** | 2000

3 x 2.2 cm
Lampworked, raked; dots, Satake glass
Photo by artist

▲ Untitled | 2002

    4.5 x 3.3 cm
Lampworked, raked; dots, Satake glass

Photo by artist

" I love the many repeated processes through which I can reflect my images, messages, and spiritualities. I love to come up with new ideas and techniques. "

Shippo-Tsunagi | 2003 ▶

    4 x 3.3 cm
Lampworked, raked; dots, Satake glass

Photo by artist

▲ **Dancing Dragonfly** | 1999

3 x 2.7 cm
Lampworked, raked; handmade millifiori,
dots, Satake glass

Photo by artist

" I create my pieces by placing dots, then raking to express my imagination over the surface of the beads, usually without using mosaic parts and clear glass. I create other pieces by placing dots over white beads first. Then I use the images that spring up from those seemingly random placements and develop them into finished works "

Untitled | 2002 ▶

3.5 x 2.4 cm
Lampworked, raked; dots,
Satake glass

Photo by artist

▲ **Untitled** | 2006

4.5 x 3 cm
Lampworked, raked; dots,
Satake glass

Photo by artist

Donna Milliron

PÂTE DE VERRE, OR GLASS PASTE, is a kiln-forming technique in which frits and glass powders are packed into molds and heated until the glass melts together. The result is a bead with a translucent, velvet-like appearance—an effect that is unattainable in beads made on a torch. Pâte de verre was frequently used in Art Nouveau jewelry. The designs that result from the technique are often compact, with only slightly raised surface decoration.

Donna Milliron's pâte de verre beads are adventurous. Although her early beads are compact and blockish in shape like traditional pâte de verre pieces, the inclusion of wire and dichroic glass gives an edge to the otherwise homogenous translucence of the glass. Her ambitious floral designs have many raised petals and blossoms. These elevated sections are carefully planned, so the glass fills them completely and the color stays in position. Milliron achieves subtle shading by mixing clear glass powder with stronger colors to dilute their intensity. She also creates new shades by mixing colors of glass powder before pouring them into the mold.

▲ **Cityscape, Whisper, Dreamscape** | 1995
3.2 x 2.2 x 2.2 cm
Pâte de verre, faceted and shaped; dichroic glass, niobium wire, soda-lime glass
Photo by Christopher Marchetti

" One of the draws of
working with a kiln
and with molds is that
you never know what
you are going to end up
with. Opening the kiln
after cooling is a lot like
Christmas morning—either
you get that thing you really
hoped you would get, or
you end up with another
pair of socks. "

◀ **Flower Geode** | 1998
4.4 x 3.8 x 2.5 cm
Lampworked, pâte de verre; 22-kt gold foil,
soda-lime glass
Photo by artist

▲ **Whispers Necklace** | 1994

4.4 x 3.5 x .9 cm
Pâte de verre, lampworked, heat and gravity shaped; etched;
dichroic glass, niobium wire, soda-lime glass

Photo by artist

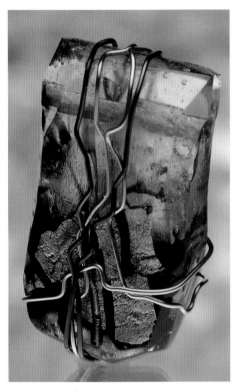

▲ **Crystal** | 1997

4.1 x 2.8 x 1.3 cm
Pâte de verre, faceted and shaped; dichroic
glass, niobium wire, soda-lime glass

Photo by Christopher Marchetti

▲ **Untitled** | 1998

6.4 x 3.2 x 1.3 cm
Pâte de verre, shaped; dichroic glass;
niobium wire; soda-lime glass

Photo by Christopher Marchetti

" I have always been fascinated by the fact that glass
is so fragile, and yet we find ancient pieces still
intact. Since beads were the first thing made with
glass, my participation in this art form feels like I'm
connecting the past with the present and the future.
It gives me a spiritual kick. "

DONNA MILLIRON

▲ **Strong Woman** | 1999

   5.1 x 2.2 x 1.3 cm
   Pâte de verre, shaped; dichroic glass, gold and silver foils, anodized
   niobium, seed beads, soda-lime glass

   Photo by artist

▲ **Floral Bead** | 1998

3.8 x 3.8 x 1.3 cm
Lampworked, pâte de verre; soda-lime-glass
Photo by artist

▼ **Floral Bead** | 1999

3.8 cm in diameter
Lampworked, pâte de verre;
soda-lime glass
Photo by artist

◀ **Floral Bead** | 2000

3.8 cm in diameter
Lampworked, pâte de verre; 22-kt gold foil,
soda-lime glass
Photo by artist

▲ **Floral Bead** | 2005

3.8 cm in diameter
Lampworked, pâte de verre; 22-kt gold
foil, soda-lime glass

Photo by artist

" Kiln work is a cerebral way to form glass, in that you have to plan it all out, then add the heat, and hope you planned well. Other forms are more kinetic and direct, involving more real-time, direct manipulation that doesn't necessarily require planning. "

▲ Floral Bead | 2002

3.8 cm in diameter
Lampworked, pâte de verre; 22-kt gold foil, soda-lime glass
Photo by artist

Harold Williams Cooney

A BEAD IS COMMONLY DEFINED as a round object with a hole running through its center. However, very little is common about the beads made by Harold Williams Cooney. A great deal is unexpected, including his choice of borosilicate glass—a material that has a slightly unsavory reputation due to its use by lampwork pipemakers.

Cooney's colors are bold, strong, and frequently opaque. He avoids the muted, milky colors often associated with borosilicate beads. His use of multi-colored latticino and murrini are direct references to the flamboyant goblets and chandeliers of Murano, Italy. While Cooney does create conventional beads, he also produces a large number of pendants. To create a pendant, he forms and decorates the bead on the end of a rod or punty. When the bead is finished and still in the flame, he adds the pendant loop, then he removes the finished bead from the punty.

◀ **Hollow-Blown Flat-Backed Raked Stringer Pendant with Marbles** | 2004

6.3 x 4.5 x 1.7 cm
Lampworked, silver fumed, wrapped, raked, hollow blown, pulled, sandblasted; marbles, bails, borosilicate glass

Photo by Joanie Beldin

▼ Organic Contemporary Chevron Attempt | 2006

Left: 4.5 x 1.2 x 1.2 cm; right: 2.4 x 1.8 x 1.8 cm
Solid work, hollow work, coldwork, hollow blown, pulled,
cut; canes, borosilicate glass

Photo by Joanie Beldin

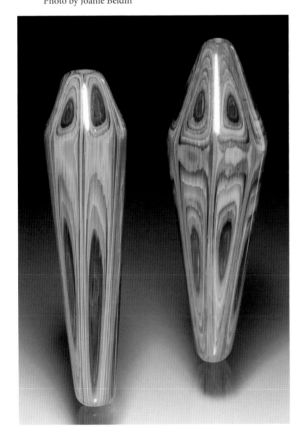

▲ Hollow-Blown Flat-Backed Raked Stringer Bead | 2004

5.8 x 5.8 x .8 cm
Lampworked, silver fumed, wrapped, raked, hollow-blown, sandblasted, borosilicate glass

Photo by Joanie Beldin

▲ **Murrini Pick-up Pendant** │ 2000

    4.4 x 3.5 x .9 cm

    Pulled; shaped; murrini, canes, borosilicate glass

    Photo by Joanie Beldin

Wide-Band Hollow-Blown Zanfirico Pendant │ 2005 ▶

    7.2 x 4.8 x .8 cm

    Cut, shaped, blown; latticino, borosilicate glass

    Photo by Joanie Beldin

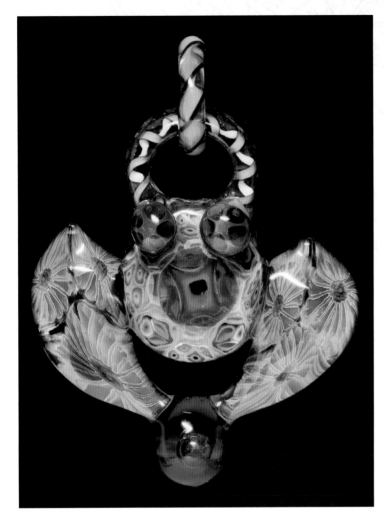

◀ **Last Place Pendant** │ 2002

7.3 x 5.4 x 1 cm
Bail, latticino, borosilicate glass
Photo by Joanie Beldin

" Glass has shown me who I am and where,

in a history far greater than myself, I stand. "

▲ **Tumbled Organic Pendant** │ 2001

    3.5 x 2.5 x 1.5 cm

    Cold work, layered, tumbled; borosilicate glass

    Photo by Joanie Beldin

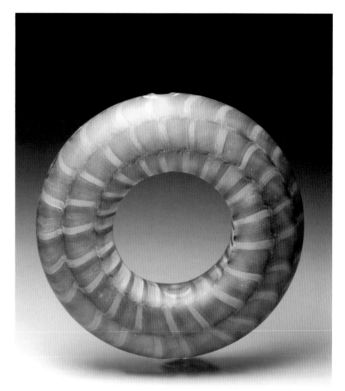

▲ **Five-Holer Hollow-Blown Coil Doughnut Bead** │ 2005

    6.2 x 6.2 x 1.2 cm

    Blown, flame polished; solid rod, borosilicate glass

    Photo by Joanie Beldin

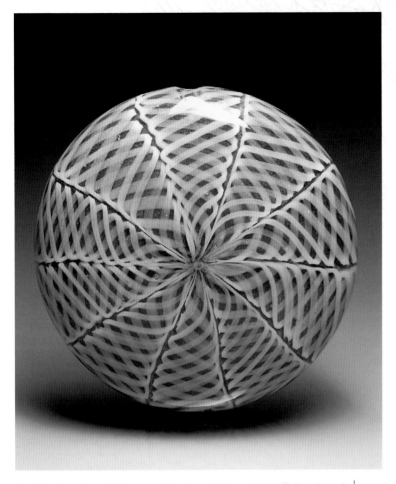

▲ Five by Ten White and Spring Colored Zanfirico Bead | 2004

5 x 5 x .8 cm
Cut, shaped, blown; latticino, borosilicate glass

Photo by Joanie Beldin

" At the moment you read this, someone somewhere is thinking that the piece of glass they are about to finish will be fit to stand tall against the material's history of more than a thousand years. "

" In my world, the word "master" is, for lack of a better name, holy. After seven years as a lampworker, I don't consider myself a glass master, although my goal is to one day become one. "

▲ Rescue Bead | 2004

2.5 x 2.5 x 1 cm
Layered, marvered, rolled, encased; borosilicate glass
Photo by Joanie Beldin

▲ Shifty Bead | 2001

3 x 3 x 1.3 cm

Decorated, striped, pulled, nubbed, blown, twisted, shaped; borosilicate glass

Photo by Joanie Beldin

▲ Black and White Zanfirico Pendant | 2006

7.5 x 4.8 x 1 cm

Zanfirico, pulled, tapered; borosilicate glass

Photo by Joanie Beldin

Terri Caspary Schmidt

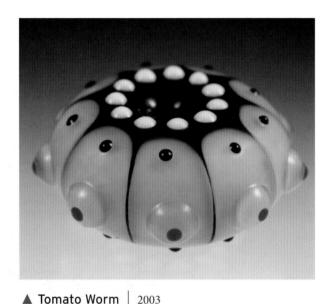

▲ **Tomato Worm** | 2003

3 x 1.6 cm
Lampworked, heat and gravity shaped, layered;
soda-lime glass

Photo by Margot Geist

PATTERNS ARE CENTRAL to the work of
Terri Caspary Schmidt. The fluid properties of
hot glass, including surface tension and viscosity,
encourage the formation of rectangles, hexagons,
and other polygons on her beads. Schmidt
applies dots to the surface of her beads, paying
careful attention to placement and volume. The
polygon shapes form as the dots are melted into
the surface of each bead. The spaces between the
dots are compressed into very thin lines. These
lines are a critical part of Schmidt's aesthetic.
Schmidt employs the repetition of some of
the most basic techniques in bead making to
transform simple, orderly patterns into designs
of challenging complexity. For instance, the
parade of small winged creatures that march
around the center of her bead "Birds" is the
product of exacting—even tedious—marvering,
picking, and re-melting. Whether simple or
complex, Schmidt's patterns are so clearly seen
and finely made, it seems that after the first dot is
placed, the rest of the pattern is inevitable.

▼ **Untitled** | 2006

3.9 x 2.2 cm
Lampworked, heat and gravity shaped, layered;
soda-lime glass

Photo by Margot Geist

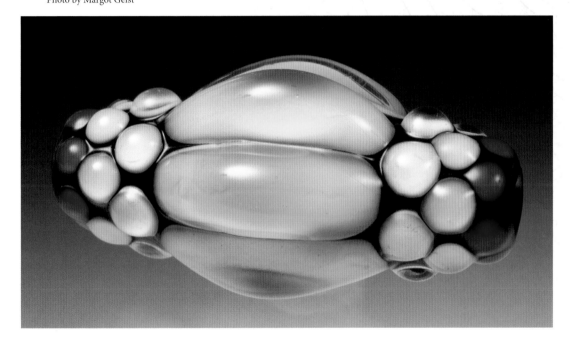

" Lampworking is like playing an instrument or speaking a foreign language. Practice, repetition, and mastery of technique bring the satisfaction of being able to fully express a wider range of ideas. I find that if I spend too much time away from the torch, I have to reacquaint myself with the language of the glass. "

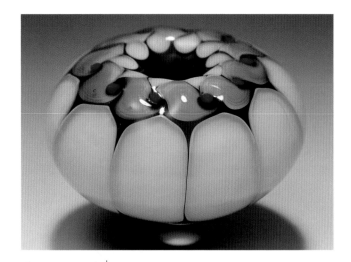

▲ **Lotus Pod** | 2004

2.9 x 1.6 cm

Lampworked, heat and gravity shaped, layered; soda-lime glass

Photo by Margot Geist

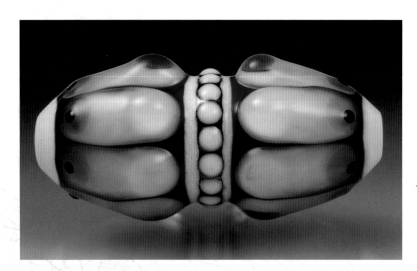

◄ **Untitled** | 2006

4.5 x 1.9 cm

Lampworked, heat and gravity shaped, layered, marvered; soda-lime glass

Photo by Margot Geist

▼ **Trillium** | 2006

2.4 x 2 cm
Lampworked, heat and gravity shaped;
soda-lime glass

Photo by Margot Geist

" Inspiration can be found in unexpected ways. I've always been attracted
to textile and architectural design elements as well as botanical,
marine, and microscopic life forms. Sometimes I find that the best
ideas can be derived from simply working with the glass itself. I like
how ideas emerge and develop from deep concentration on a particular
lampworking technique. "

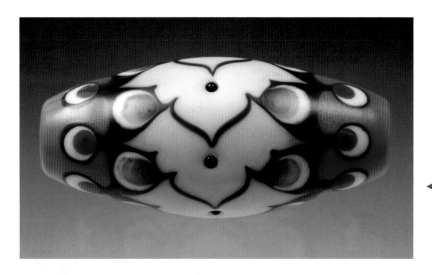

◀ **Moroccan** | 2006

4.1 x 1.3 cm
Lampworked, heat and gravity shaped;
soda-lime glass
Photo by Margot Geist

◀ **Moroccan** | 2006

4 x 1.8 cm
Lampworked, heat and gravity shaped;
soda-lime glass
Photo by Margot Geist

▲ Birds | 2006

3.7 x 1.9 cm
Lampworked, heat and gravity shaped,
layered and masked; soda-lime glass

Photo by Margot Geist

▼ Birds II | 2005

3.8 x 1.8 cm
Lampworked, heat and gravity shaped, acid-
etched; soda-lime glass

Photo by Margot Geist

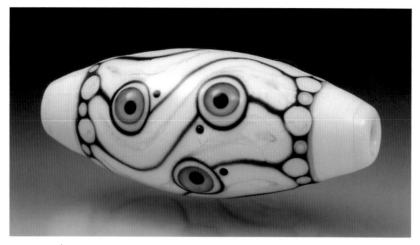

▲ **Eyes** | 2005

4.4 x 1.7 cm
Lampworked, heat and gravity shaped, marvered;
soda-lime glass

Photo by Margot Geist

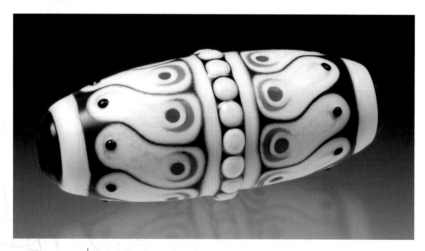

▲ **Untitled** | 2006

4.4 x 1.9 cm
Lampworked, heat and gravity shaped, marvered;
soda-lime glass

Photo by Margot Geist

▲ **Dotted Caterpillar** | 2005

3 x 1.6 cm
Lampworked, heat and gravity shaped, layered;
soda-lime glass

Photo by Margot Geist

Pati Walton

THE MINIATURE WORLDS THAT COME TO LIFE IN PATI WALTON'S BEADS are built up layer by layer. Each thin sheet of transparent glass magnifies the image below it. As the number of layers increases, an illusion of great depth is created. Between the layers, dots and small chips of cane form small fish, ribbed cane becomes sea grass, and star canes turn into anemones.

In Walton's landscape beads, these same dots and canes evolve into meadow scenes with colorful wildflowers and mountains in the distance. The butterflies that float above these meadows are murrini slices from complex figural canes. By layering and shading with hand-mixed fine stringers of glass, Walton creates miniature scenes that capture the beauty and colors of nature. Her work demonstrates that, in the end, bead making is an incremental process, as each piece is built up step by step, layer by layer.

◀ **Cardinal** | 2003

4.8 x 4.8 x 2 cm
Formed off-mandrel, encased,
polished, ground

Photo by artist

▲ **Eight Ladies** | 2003

4.8 x 4.8 x 2 cm
Formed off-mandrel; encased,
polished, ground

Photo by artist

▲ **Sunset Over the Pond** | 2006

　　4.8 x 4.8 x 1.8 cm
　　Formed off-mandrel, encased

　　Photo by artist

Mountain Bead | 1994 ▶

　　4 x 2.8 x 2.8 cm
　　Lampworked, encased; stringers, mille-
　　fiore, dichroic glass

　　Photo by artist

▲ **Irises** │ 2001

4.3 x 3.3 x 1.5 cm
Lampworked with murrini

Photo by Azad

" The foundation of my work is using multiple layers of glass to give an illusion of great depth. With my method of layering glass of different colors and transparencies, I can paint scenery in between the layers with very fine stringers of glass. The effect gives a startling illusion of background, foreground, and middle ground. "

Encased Flower │ 2002 ▶

4.5 x 4 x 2.5 cm
Lampworked, encased; dichroic glass,murrini

Photo by artist

PATI WALTON

" I have always had a huge fascination with glass. The fact that a whole world can be seen in a small paperweight, and the possibility that I could achieve something like that in my work has always been my incentive for me. After all these years, I'm still exploring the possibilities of creating a perfect bead. "

▲ Pete's Pond | 2006
5 x 5 x 1.8 cm
Formed off-mandrel, encased
Photo by artist

▲ Wonderland | 2006
5 x 5 x 1.8 cm
Formed off-mandrel, encased
Photo by artist

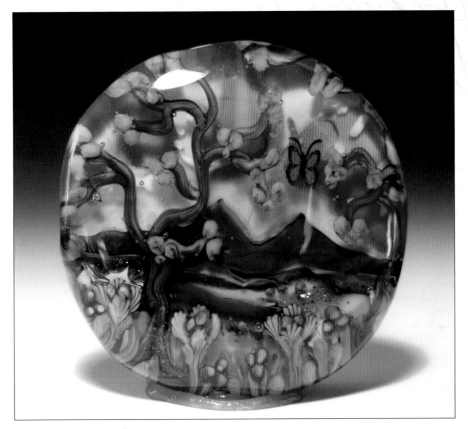

▲ **Tree Butterfly** │ 2006

4.9 x 4.9 x 1.7 cm
Formed off-mandrel, encased

Photo by artist

▲ **Dolphin** │ 1994

4 x 3 x 3 cm
Lampworked; stringers
Photo by artist

" My landscape scenes and aquarium
beads were real breakthroughs,
because I could finally give the beads
the depth and imagery I wanted.
These beads posed the artistic
challenge of trying to capture the
beauty and colors of nature. By
layering and shading with hand-
mixed fine stringers of glass, I was
able to create miniature scenes that
said, "Jump right in." "

▲ **Square Aquarium** | 2005

    3.8 x 4.5 x 1.1 cm

    Formed off-mandrel, encased, ground, polished

    Photo by artist

▲ **Aquarium Bead** | 2001

    3.6 x 3 x 2.2 cm

    Lampworked; dichroic glass, stringers, murrini

    Photo by Azad

René Roberts

SOMEWHERE IN THE UNIVERSE, ON SOME DISTANT PLANET, there must be a beach where the pebbles resemble the beads made by René Roberts. Like metamorphic rocks, Roberts' beads have been randomly altered by heat. This effect is achieved when sheets of metal leaf are rolled onto the hot surface of glass beads. The results are both predictable and unpredictable. The basic chemical reactions take place, but the nuances of the final patterns and colors occur from happenstance. The range of colors is conventional, but the hues are not. Heat, time, and the chemistry of the flame itself all factor into the result.

In addition to remarkable color, Roberts' beads feature geometric elements that resemble the glyphs and runes from some ancient, remote land. The beads are at once familiar and suggestive, irresistible yet unreadable. It's easy to imagine a collection of them in a home on that distant planet.

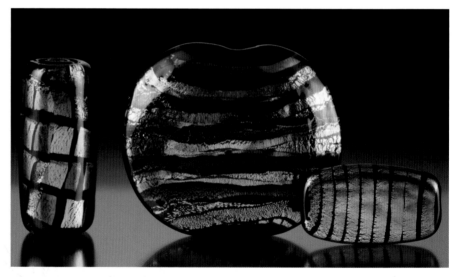

▲ **Dichroics: Mosaic Cylinder, Lenticular Tablet, Rainbow Tablet** │ 1993
Tablet: 3 x 4 x 1 cm
Flameworked, kiln fused, press-molded; dichroic soda-lime sheet glass
Photo by artist

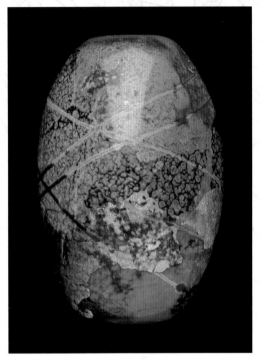

▲ **Variations on Moss Beads** | 1993–1999

Varied dimensions
Flameworked, press molded, tumbled; copper, silver
and gold leaf, iron oxide, enamel, soda-lime glass

Main photo by artist
Detail by George Post

❝ It's ironic that many fine objects that are celebrated
as "handcrafted" are displayed with prominent signs
that say "Do Not Touch"—admonitions that discourage
any kind of tactile interaction. One of the attractions
of beads is that they're made to be handled, to be
experienced by touch as well as sight. There's an
intimacy to them that few other media share. ❞

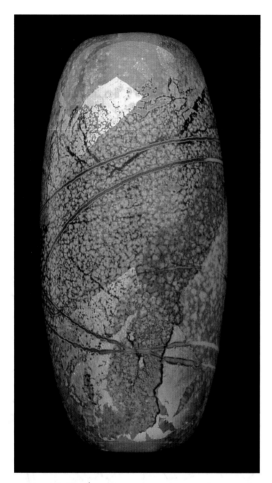

▲ **Ice Moss** | 1995

4.5 cm in length
Flameworked; copper, silver, 24-k gold,
soda-lime glass

Photo by George Post

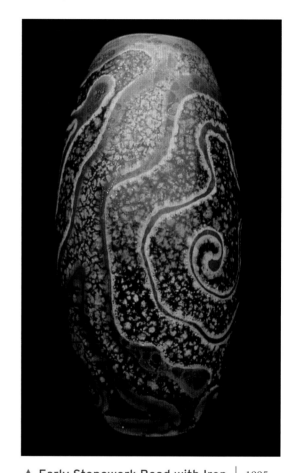

▲ **Early Stonework Bead with Iron** | 1995

5.5 cm in length
Flameworked, etched, tumbled; copper and
silver leaf, iron oxide, soda-lime glass

Photo by George Post

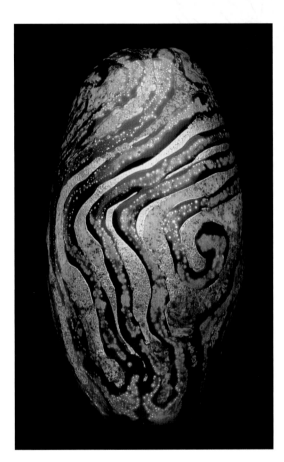

◀ **Atlantis** │ 1996

4 cm in length
Flameworked, torch reduced; silver, copper, and gold
leaf, iron oxide, soda-lime glass

Photo by George Post 1053

" I love the subtle color schemes in nature: fresh
seaweed on sand, lichen on stone. From the
beginning, I searched for ways to achieve these
subtle colors in my work and to create a look to the
glass that was more like a natural material. "

Bronzed Beads with Red │ 2002 ▶

Longest: 4 cm
Flameworked, blown, bronze, silver, gold
leaf, soda-lime glass

Photo by artist

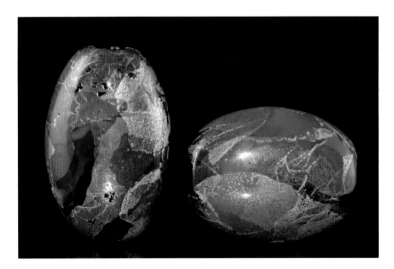

" I grew up on a beach in Southern California. As a child I remember looking at the sand and noticing that each grain was a different color. My work has never been far from that landscape. It's imprinted in my work—in the materials, the colors, the patterns, the tension between randomness and order. "

▲ **Stonework Beads and Variations** | 1995–2001

Longest: 6 cm
Lampworked, iridized, fumed, etched, tumbled; copper, silver, gold, iron, enamels, soda-lime glass
Photo by Hap Sakwa

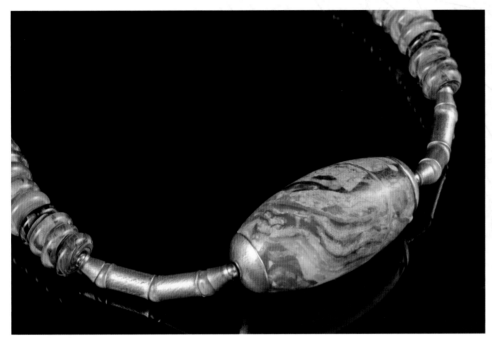 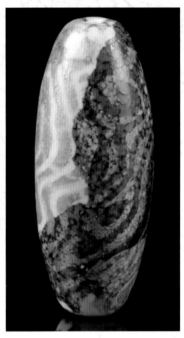

▲ **Aerial Views** | 1996

Longest: 6 cm

Flameworked, tumbled; copper, silver, gold, soda-lime glass

Main photo by artist
Detail by George Post

▲ **Confetti Gold Beads** | 1996–1999

Tallest: 4 cm
Flameworked; gold and silver leaf,
soda-lime glass

Photo by artist

Nebula Black Necklace | 2003 ▶

Bead: 5 cm in length
Flameworked; gold and silver leaf, blown
glass shards, soda-lime glass

Photo by Hap Sakwa

RENÉ ROBERTS

◀ **Tall Nebula Vessels** │ 2002

Tallest: 6 cm
Flameworked, acid etched; gold and silver
leaf, blown glass shards, soda-lime glass

Photo by artist

**Amethyst Lake Vessel and Oval
Lenticular Tablet** │ 2002 ▶

Vessel: 4.5 cm tall
Flameworked, iridized, fumed; copper
and gold leaf, silver foil, soda-lime glass

Photo by artist

Hiroko Hayashi-Kogure

THE FACT THAT BEADS ARE MADE TO BE WORN is part of what drew Hiroko Hayashi-Kogure to bead making. Initially, she worked with fabric and textiles as a weaver and knitter. Once she started making beads, the patterns and color, regularity and spontaneity of traditional Japanese textile design had a visible impact on her work. The crisply outlined patterns on her beads are like block printing on cloth. Her more elaborate designs resemble the silk embroidery on classic kimonos.

Adornment is a matter of taste, subject to the whims of the current vogue. What is popular today is ancient history tomorrow. Hayashi-Kogure's references to traditional fabric patterns unite her beads to a wider world of color and design. Her choice of timeless patterns ensures that her beads will outlive any fashion movement.

◄ Hana-Monyou | 2006

2.5 x 2 cm
Lampworked, raked; dots, twisty and handmade murrini; soda-lime glass
Photo by Takayuki Matsuzawa

▲ **Various "Warring States" Beads** │ 1999–2006

Each: 2.2 x 1.8 cm
Lampworked, etched; dots, stringers, soda-lime glass
Photo by Takayuki Matsuzawa

◀ **Seven-Eye Bead** | 1998

2 x 2 cm
Lampworked, etched; soda-lime glass
Photo by artist

▲ **Tasuki-Wa-Monyou** | 2001

1.7 x 2 cm
Lampworked; dots, striped cane,
stringers, soda-lime glass
Photo by artist

▲ **Pattern Like Mosaic** | 2006

1.8 x 2.2 cm
Lampworked, etched, raked, dots stringers,
twisty and handmade murrini, soda-lime glass
Photo by artist

▲ Saiiki | 2005

1.9 x 2.1 cm
Lampworked, raked; gold leaf, dots,
stringer, twisty and handmade murrini, soda-lime glass
Photo by artist

" My influences include Japanese culture—the tea ceremony, the kimono, bonsai, Noh attire, old temples, and gardens. All of these things have certainly influenced me. I have always been fascinated by antique beads. Now I am also fascinated by the inventiveness and the free-minded designs of American artists. "

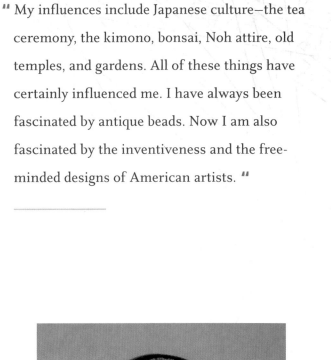

Feather Stitch | 2002 ▶

2.1 x 2.5 cm
Lampworked, raked, dichroic
coating, dots, soda-lime glass
Photo by artist

▲ An Ancient Necklace | 1997

Largest: 2 x 2.4 cm; 65 cm long
Lampworked; soda-lime glass
Photo by artist

" It seems that wearing necklaces was popular in ancient Japan until the development of kimono culture. Now I would like to produce attractive adornments to complement the kimono. "

▲ **Ko-Imari** | 2006

    2 x 2 cm

    Lampworked; stringers, striped cane and twisty,
soda-lime glass

    Photo by artist

Untitled | 1997 ▶

    1.5 x 2 cm

    Lampworked; silver leaf, soda-lime glass

    Photo by artist

▲ **Encased Rope** │ 1999

2.1 x 2.2 cm
Lampworked; lead glass, soda-lime glass;

Photo by artist

▲ Banded Mosaic Beads | 1999

Largest: 1.2 x 4 cm
Lampworked; soda-lime glass
Photo by artist

" Prior to working with glass, I worked with naturally dyed cloth, textile fabrics, weaving, and kilting. I can see influences in my glass work from those experiences with different color combinations and patterns. The reason I fell in love with glass beads is because they're wearable—they're not just displayed on a shelf. "

Loren Stump

THE GLASS PORTRAIT CANE, A 19TH-CENTURY VENETIAN CURIOSITY, has been reinvigorated in the work of Loren Stump. Stump creates elaborate murrini to use as built-in sections for his portraits. The eyes, nose, and mouth of each face are made separately, pulled down to size, and then assembled into a finished portrait. A thin slice of the complete face is added to the surface of a bead to create a glass portrait.

Murrini add detail to Stump's sculptural beads. They become the drivers and passengers in beads that resemble diminutive cars. They become the mermaids and dolphins inside his diorama seashells. Stump also carves realistic animal heads and animal figures based on Japanese ivory ojime into hot glass. His Baby Rhino bead, for example, is a baby rhinoceros wearing drop-seat pajamas decorated with Mickey Mouse faces. This combination of remarkable skill and popular culture is classic Loren Stump.

◀ **Taxi and Police Cars** │ 2002

2.5 x 3.2 x 2.5 cm
Lampworked, sculpted, encased murrini, soda-lime glass

Photos by Rich Images

▲ **Rat Ojime Bead** | 1995

2.5 x 2.5 x 2.6 cm
Lampworked, sculpted, tea-stained; soda-lime glass

Photo by Rich Images

▼ Golden Rose Mardi-Gras Mask │ 2006

6.3 x 4.4 x 1.2 cm
Lampworked; sculpted murrini, soda-lime glass
Photo by David Poinsett

" Glass is the material of choice for me. It does not want to
be controlled; therefore, it forces me to want to control it. I
know that perfection in glass can never be achieved, and that
satisfaction is all one can hope for. "

▲ **Baby Rhino** | 2006

6.4 x 3.8 x 3.9 cm
Lampworked sculpted; soda-lime glass, murrini

Photo by Takayuki Matsuzawa

▲ **Marie in Blue** | 2001

5.5 x 3.5 x 2.4 cm
Lampworked, sculpted; soda-lime glass

Photo by David Poinsett

◀ **Tiger Head Pendant** | 2005

5.1 x 5.4 x 2.5 cm
Lampworked, sculpted; soda-lime glass

Photo by David Poinsett

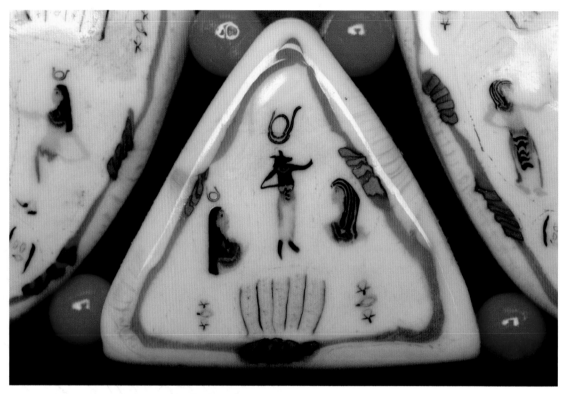

▲ **Egyptian Cartouche Collar** | 1995

Necklace: 45.7 cm
Lampworked; tapered tablets, murrini overlay,
soda-lime glass

Photo by Rich Images

" I began lampworking in 1993, after twenty-three years in the stained glass industry. I have the benefit of being self-taught—no one told me what I could not achieve. At its best, art is what you are driven to do. It comes from inspiration within, not from a preconceived idea of what it should be. "

◀ Horse Ojime Bead | 2005

4.5 x 2.5 x 1.9 cm
Lampworked, sculpted, tea-stained;
soda-lime glass

Photos by Rich Images

LOREN STUMP

5.4 x 3.8 x 3.9 cm
Lampworked, sculpted, coldworked; soda-lime glass, layered murrini

Photo by David Poinsett

▲ Golden Egg | 2006

5.2 x 3.1 x 2.6 cm
Lampworked, coldworked, vacuum encased; butterfly murrini, gold leaf, soda-lime glass

Photo by Rich Images

Paperweight Pendant | 2006 ▶

3.8 x 1.6 cm
Lampworked, vacuum encased; dichroic, soda-lime glass, butterfly murrini

Photo by Takayuki Matsuzawa

LOREN STUMP

" In glass, you learn more from failures than success. Therefore, it isn't what you can make—it is what you can fix. It is not how many beads you can create in an hour—it is how good you can make one single bead. "

▲ Madonna Button | 2005

2.8 x 2.5 x .6 cm
Lampworked; murrini, soda-lime glass
Photo by Rich Images

James Allen Jones

▲ **Untitled** | 2004

3.5 x 1.5 cm
Lampworked, press textured; soda-lime glass,
sifted enamels

Photo by Joanie Beldin

MURRINI ARE THIN SLICES of patterned glass canes that have been pulled to reduce the size of the designs. These canes are usually made in a hot shop using metal optic molds. They can also be built up layer by layer at the torch. However, Jim Jones uses a technique called bundling to make his murrini. He begins by arranging small, thin pieces of sheet glass into a complex pattern called a bundle. This bundle is held in place with a loop of wire, then brought up to temperature and stretched to reduce and sharpen the pattern, and create the desired diameter. After cooling, the cane is sliced into the murrini.

The technique of bundling has allowed Jones to ingeniously arrange his glass sheets so that they have a space in the center. When the canes are pulled, the hole remains. Murrini from these canes can be slipped over the end of a mandrel to form a continuous design around the hole of the bead. Jones' mosaic beads are planned with precision, so that the kaleidoscopic pattern covers the entire surface of the bead in a uniform fashion.

" Beads seem like small messages from the past to the future. The message is that it's important to humans of this age to make and share beautiful things. Shell beads made 100,000 years ago tell us something about our similarities to the people who made them."

▲ **Untitled** │ 1999
   3.5 x 3 x 2.5 cm
   Lampworked; silver leaf; soda-lime glass
   Photo by Joanie Beldin

▲ **Untitled** | 1998

Left: 1.5 cm x 2 x 2 cm; right: 2 x 2.5 x 2.5 cm

Lampworked, cold-bundled murrini and endcaps,
sifted and rolled enamel, silver foils, soda-lime glass
Photo by artist

" I enjoy the immediate aspects of exploring and inventing

a bead design as it happens. My work as a bead maker is

grounded in the pleasure of invention and the discipline of

concentration. To make mosaic beads, I work in a precise,

disciplined way, creating complex bundles that require

detailed planning to design. "

JAMES ALLEN JONES

▲ **Untitled** | 1999

Left: 2.5 x 3 x 3; right: 2.8 x 3.3 x 3.3 cm
Lampworked, marvered, tumbled; cold-bundled
murrini, latticino, soda-lime glass

Photo by artist

Untitled | 1997–2006 ▶

Left: 2 x 2.2 x 2; right: 2.3 x 1.8 x 1.8 cm
Lampworked, marvered; cold-bundled
murrini and endcaps, soda-lime glass

Photo by Joanie Beldin

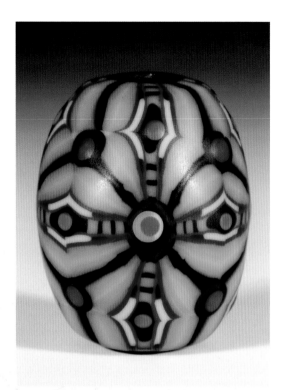

> " I made my early beads with strips of sheet glass, because it was readily available. Using sheet glass led me to develop cold-bundle glory-hole techniques for the production of the murrinis, hollow glass cane, and mosaic end caps for which my early beads became known. "

▲ **Untitled** | 2004

3.5 x 2 x 2 cm
Lampworked, marvered; cold-bundled
murrini and endcaps, soda-lime glass

Photo by Joanie Beldin

▲ **Untitled** | 2000

1.6 x 2 x 2 cm
Lampworked, marvered, tumbled; cold-bundled
murrini and endcaps, soda-lime glass

Photo by artist

JAMES ALLEN JONES

▲ **Untitled** | 1996–2006

Left: 2.3 x 1.5 x 1.5; right: 1.8 x 2.2 x 2.2
Lampworked; marvered; cold-bundled murrini and
endcaps, soda-lime glass

Photo by Joanie Beldin

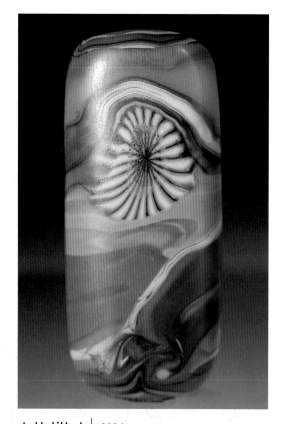

▲ **Untitled** | 2006

2.1 x 2.1 cm

Lampworked, marvered, pressed, tumbled; soda-lime glass

Photo by artist

▲ **Untitled** | 1995

3 x 2 cm

Lampworked; cold-bundled murrini and endcaps, soda-lime glass

Photo by Joanie Beldin

▲ **Untitled** | 2006

2.4 x 2 x 2 cm

Lampworked, marvered; cold-bundled murrini and endcaps, soda-lime glass

Photo by artist

▲ **Untitled** | 2003

2.7 x 2.2 x 2 cm

Lampworked, clear cased; soda-lime glass, stringer, silver leaf

Photo by artist

HOLLAND

Sage Holland

THE BEADS OF SAGE HOLLAND have a distinct talismanic quality. They are like tokens and totems designed for modern life, but they have clear references to the past. Symbols from ancient civilizations as well as sacred references to other cultures often appear in Holland's work.

Holland frequently uses the Egyptian Eye symbol in her designs. She does this in acknowledgement of the Eye's power as an icon and in tribute to the significance of Egypt in the history of glass working. She uses striped disks to make her Islamic folded beads, reinterpreting this ancient technique and making a minimum number of folds. Holland's double-disk folded beads wave like fabric in the wind. Her large disk and star beads have a pattern that starts in the center and radiates outward like a Tibetan mandala.

▲ **Yin Yang and the 4 Directions** | 2000

3 x 3 x .8 cm
Lampworked, feathered; side glancing dots, murrini, soft glass
Photo by Tom Holland

When Two Paths Meet | 2006 ▶

4.2 x 3.4 x 1.1 cm
Lampworked, layered, feathered, spiraled; sideglancing dots, soft glass
Photo by Tom Holland

▲ Dancing in Polka Dots | 1999

4.3 x 2 x 1 cm
Lampworked; murrini face, manipulated stringers and dots, soft glass

Photo by Tom Holland

" There is a sense of fulfillment in the subtle rhythm of the heating, winding, and shaping of molten glass. The process can be a deeply introspective path of self-discovery and meditation. I rejoice in creating beads as tokens of mind and matter, as talismanic objects that speak to the primal core of our human roots. **"**

" A bead is small yet profound, a sort of time capsule with communicative value. I view bead making as a form of cultural cross-pollination. On a rare occasion, while digging in the garden, I'll unearth an ancient arrowhead or spearhead. I hope one day in the distant future someone will find one of my beads while digging in his or her garden. "

▲ **Lucky Devil** | 1999

4.3 x 3.5 x .9 cm
Lampworked; flattened and decorated; stringers, dots, murrini; soft glass
Photo by Tom Holland

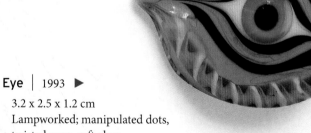

Eye | 1993 ▶

3.2 x 2.5 x 1.2 cm
Lampworked; manipulated dots, twisted cane, soft glass
Photo by Fred Sears

▲ **Snake Necklace** | 2004

62 x 3.3 x 1 cm
Lampworked; stacked feathered dots,
soft glass

Photo by Robert K. Lui/Ornament

▼ **Cross** | 2006

6.3 x 1.2 x 1.2 cm
Lampworked; silvered ivory and amber,
dots, soft glass

Photo by Robert K. Lui/Ornament

▲ **Wave Wheel** | 2006

6.1 x 6.1 x 1.4 cm
Lampworked, layered, spiraled; etched;
soft glass, dots

Photo by Robert K. Lui/Ornament

▲ **Heron** | 2006

4.5 x 2.3 x 1.1 cm
Lampworked; frits, opaques, opalinos, feathered dots, stringers, soft glass

Photo by Robert K. Lui/Ornament

▲ **Stratified Star** | 2005

4.4 x 4.4 x .9 cm
Lampworked, layered, stacked dots,
soft glass

Photo by Robert K. Lui/Ornament

" I'm captivated by the relationship between illuminated color and pattern. I often seek harmony in the use of symmetry in my work—it helps me find order in the chaos. The control of a simple dab of hot glass can lead to unlimited variations, some as ancient as glass itself, and some yet to be discovered! "

◄ **Prayer Scroll** │ 2006
3.1 x 4.7 x 1.5 cm
Lampworked; dots, stringers, joined beads, soft glass
Photos by Robert K. Lui/Ornament

▲ **Dutchman's Britches** │ 2006

3.3 x 3.5 x 2.5 cm
Lampworked, folded, pinched, stretched, etched,
layered; soft glass

Photo by Robert K. Lui/Ornament

Pat Frantz

DICHROIC GLASS IS A TECHNOLOGICAL INNOVATION in which incredibly thin layers of metal oxide vapors are coated onto the surface of a glass sheet. Like butterfly wings, dichroic glass reflects one color and transmits another. The glass is beautiful but also notoriously difficult to work with. Working the glass in a flame without disfiguring its fragile coating can be challenging. Thanks to its beauty, dichroic glass can easily overwhelm a design.

Pat Frantz is unfazed by these obstacles. She wholeheartedly embraces the color, shine, and splendor of dichroic glass. She often heaps colors, patterns, and textures onto a single bead, and the end effect is exuberant. There is nothing tame about her work, although it isn't completely without order or restraint. Straightforward, clearly outlined designs keep the exotic nature of the dichroic glass under control.

Tabular Bead with Multi Layers of Dichroic Glass | 1995 ▶

3.5 x 2.5 x .8 cm
Marvered, flattened, paddle shaped; dichroic glass, black soda-lime glass
Photo by Keith Hobbs

▲ **Flat Multi-Layered Dichroic Pendant Bead** │ 2005

4 x 3.5 x .5 cm
Layered, dichroic coated, pinched, marvered, smoothed,
flattened; soda-lime glass

Photo by Keith Hobbs

◀ **Yellow and Blue Feathered Bead with Red Dichroic Encasement** | 2001

4 x 2 x 2 cm

Dichroic coated, paddle shaped, feathered, soda-lime glass

Photo by Keith Hobbs

◀ **Long Multi-Colored Dichroic Bicone with Raised Goldstone Detail** | 2002

4.5 x 1.5 x 1.5 cm

Dichroic coated; paddle shaped, goldstone strip, soda-lime glass

Photo by Keith Hobbs

◀ **Large Oval Multi-Layered Dichroic Bead with Milk Encasement** | 2006

4 x 2 x 2 cm
Pinched, encased and marvered smooth; black
soda-lime glass, dichroic glass
Photo by Keith Hobbs

" I've discovered that there's a huge group of people who love to buy beads—I call these loyal customers bead-a-holics. Without them, I don't think the glass bead movement would have become what it is today. I think beads are somehow embedded in human DNA, because the need to make or own beads has been so strong over the course of human history. "

PAT FRANTZ

▲ Dichroic Bicone Bead with Patterned Dichroic and
Goldstone Decorative Band | 2005

    2 x 4 x 2 cm

    Lampworked, paddle shaped, dichroic coated, soda-lime glass

    Photo by Keith Hobbs

" Inspiration for my bead designs comes from everywhere. Historical research plays a big part in the design work that I do. Seeing an ancient tribal design can trigger a series of bead designs that might not look anything like the original stimulus but was inspired by that creative source nonetheless. "

▲ Yellow and Black Feathered Bicone with
Blue Dichroic Eyes and Goldstone Details | 2002

    3.5 x 2 x 2 cm
    Paddle shaped, dichroic coated; soda-lime glass, custom
    goldstone stringers
    Photo by Keith Hobbs

◀ Blue Dichroic Tabular Bead with
Pattern Dichroic and Goldstone Detail | 2005

    .7 x 2.5 x 4 cm
    Lampworked, paddle shaped, pressed, dichroic coated;
    soda-lime glass
    Photo by Keith Hobbs

▲ **Black Bicone Bead with Pink and White Feathered Design** | 1989

2.5 x 1.5 x 1.5 cm
Paddle shaped; soda-lime glass
Photo by Keith Hobbs

Dichroic Borosilicate Bicone Bead | 2004 ▶

2 x 4 x 2 cm
Lampworked, paddle shaped; borosilicate color rod,
borosilicate dichroic-coated sheet glass
Photo by Keith Hobbs

◀ **A Heavily Silvered Olive-Shaped Bead with Blue Dichroic Bumps** | 2004

1.5 x 2.5 x 1.5 cm
Copper green soda-lime glass, silver foil, dichroic glass, black decorations

Photo by Keith Hobbs

Red Dragonfly on Dichroic Leaf | 2003 ▶

4 x 3 x 1 cm
Lampworked paddle shaped, textured, dichroic coated; soda-lime glass

Photo by Keith Hobbs

Emiko Sawamoto

▲ **Noh Mask of Hannya** | 1996
   3.8 x 2.4 x 2 cm
   Lampworked, sculpted; soda-lime glass
   Photo by Rich Images

ALTHOUGH EMIKO SAWAMOTO was born in Japan, she considers herself an American bead maker. She lives and works in America, and many of her beads make distinct references to American pop culture. Her Marilyn Monroe beads feature a sculptural version of the movie icon.

Sawamoto's pattern and murrini beads are reflections of Japanese bead design. Their colors are especially bold due to her use of Italian glass. The detailed modeling of her sculptural faces and small figures are often combined with small decorative canes. Her vibrant murrini pendant possesses the color and attitude of a 1950's movie poster. The technical challenges of the detailed work seen in Sawamoto's beads are made all the more difficult by the excessively hot torches used in American studios.

" In the beginning, I wanted to create beautiful round beads for jewelry making. Then my interest drifted toward sculptures. Although I now make more round beads than sculptural beads, I'm often referred to as a sculptural bead maker in magazines. These days, I strive to create pieces that are uniquely mine. "

▲ Spring Dream | 2003

3 x 1.8 cm
Lampworked; applied murrini, soda-lime glass
Photo by Rich Images

▼ **Flower Festival Temari** | 2000

2.4 cm in diameter
Lampworked; soda-lime glass

Photo by Rich Images

▼ **Futatsugiku Temari** | 1998

2.4 cm in diameter
Lampworked; combed ribbon canes,
soda-lime glass

Photo by Rich Images

▲ **Rainbow Temari** | 2000

2.4 cm in diameter
Lampworked; applied ribbon canes, soda-lime glass

Photo by Rich Images

▲ **Star Temari** | 1999

2.4 cm in diameter
Lampworked; applied ribbon canes, soda-lime glass

Photo by Rich Images

▲ Egyptian | 2002
4 x 1.8 cm
Lampworked; applied murrini, soda-lime glass
Photo by Rich Images

" When I started making
beads, there were no bead or
lampwork forums, where we
could ask questions about
how things were made or how
certain effects were achieved.
So I did a lot of experiments
and learned a lot from
them. Even finding out that
something didn't work was a
good discovery. A failure made
a success! "

▲ **Fiores** │ 2006

    3.2 x 2.2 cm
    Lampworked; soda-lime glass

    Photo by Takayuki Matsuzawa

Mandarin Ducks │ 2006 ▶

    2.5 x 2.4 x 1.6 cm
    Lampworked; applied murrini,
    soda-lime glass

    Photo by Takayuki Matsuzawa

▲ **Diamonds Are Girls' Best Friends** │ 2004

    3 x 2.3 x 1.2 cm

    Lampworked, sculpted; applied murrini, soda-lime
    glass, Swarovski crystals

    Photo by Rich Images

▲ **Marilyn** │ 1996

    4 x 2.3 x 2.3 cm

    Lampworked, sculpted; soda-lime glass

    Photo by artist

" I loved caricature drawing when I was in school. I would pass around caricatures of students or teachers during classes. So it was a natural development that I started to make Hollywood stars in glass. I try to be different. If some themes or styles of beads become popular, I stay away from making them. Why choose to blend in? "

▲ **Kabuki Dancer of White Lion** | 2001

    5.2 x 5 x 2.2 cm

    Lampworked, sculpted; soda-lime glass

    Photo by Rich Images

Nicole Zumkeller and Eric Seydoux

WHILE THE HISTORY OF GLASS BEAD MAKING IN EUROPE stretches back to the Iron Age, studio glass bead making was unknown there until Nicole Zumkeller and Eric Seydoux of Ver et Framboise introduced it in the mid-1990s. When they first opened their studio in Switzerland, their torches, tools, and Italian glass rods were imported from the United States. Their inspirations have often been imported as well. Japanese kimono patterns are a clear influence on their millefiori beads—pieces in which abstract floral shapes float above meadow grasses. These meadows are full of flowers, like the alpine views Zumkeller and Seydoux see from their studio windows.

While teamwork is typical in glassblowing, it's uncommon in lampworking. There is little room for two egos in the creation of a thing as small as a bead. The torch has only one driver's seat. Yet Zumkeller and Seydoux both bring something to the bead-making process. They combine their two inquisitive souls when they create.

▲ **Herba Series** | 2005

3.7 cm in length
Heat and gravity shaped; soda-lime Italian glass
Photo by Eric Seydoux

▲ **Art Nouveau Series** | 1999

4 cm in length
Soda-lime Italian glass, silver foil
Photo by Eric Seydoux

▼ **Spaceship Series** │ 1997

4 cm in diameter
Soda-lime Italian glass

Photos by Eric Seydoux

▲ **First Beads!** │ 1994

1.5 cm in length
Soda-lime Italian glass

Photo by Eric Seydoux

" I appreciate the concentration and focus required for making beads. With other media, like painting, you can have a rest, go for a walk. With bead making, you must use your total attention all the time. It is a form of meditation. "

▲ **Disk and Scales Series** | 2005

4 cm in diameter
Soda-lime Italian glass
Photo by Eric Seydoux

▲ **Herba Series** | 2003

2.4 cm in length
Soda-lime Italian glass

Photo by Eric Seydoux

▲ **Plain Herba Series** | 2000

3.5 cm in length
Heat and gravity shaped; soda-lime Italian glass

Photo by Eric Seydoux

◀ **Mini Herba Series** | 2002

2 cm in length
Soda-lime Italian glass

Photo by Eric Seydoux

▲ **Herba Series** | 2002

4 cm in length
Heat and gravity shaped; soda-lime Italian glass
Photo by Eric Seydoux

" Our students come from all over the European continent and as far away as Canada and Mexico. Speaking three or four different languages is common in our classes. It's so rewarding when one sees a student with the "Yes! I got it!" sparkle in his or her eyes. The languages and cultures may change, but the magic is always there. "

" Japanese kimonos are a major influence on our work, especially on our millefioris. We're also influenced by Chinese Warring State beads, Asao beads, other bead makers, and nature. Nature is so infinite, far more creative than any human will ever be. We spend our free time hiking and swimming, so our link with nature is vital for us. "

▲ **Kimono Series** | 2003

2 cm in length
Soda-lime Italian glass
Photo by Eric Seydoux

Herba Series | 2006 ▶

3 cm in length
Heat and gravity shaped;
soda-lime Italian glass
Photo by Eric Seydoux

▲ Pebble Nature Series | 2006

3.8 cm in length
Soda-lime Italian glass, silver foil, semi-precious stones
Photo by Eric Seydoux

Dan Adams

WHILE TRIBAL CULTURE IS AT THE CENTER OF DAN ADAMS' BEADS, he is not in the business of making replicas. His beads draw heavily on the dot and line designs that are commonly associated with tribal decoration, but they also feature a subtle twist that makes them modern.

Adams has created diamond lozenges with the sort of raised, stratified eyes usually seen on spherical beads. His long, barrel-shaped beads have intentionally offset eyes, which create a jaunty, slightly unsettled effect. Adams uses enamel powders to create soft, mottled colors that are outside the palette of most tribal art. His beads are made to be worn. Most of his pieces are modest in size and meant to be used in strands with beads of similar design. Adams and his wife, polymer artist Cynthia Toops, frequently collaborate on long strands and finished jewelry in which polymer and glass beads play complementary roles.

◄ **Head Beads** | 1997–1998
Left: 3.2 x 1.9 x .9 cm; right: 1.9 x 1.9 x .9 cm
Lampworked, hot sculpted; enamel; soda-lime glass
Photo by Roger Schreiber

▲ **Tabular Crosses** | 2006

Left: 3.5 x 2.9 x .9 cm; center: 5.3 x 4.7 x .8 cm;
right: 4.3 x 4.8 x .9 cm
Lampworked, marvered, trail decorated; soda-lime
glass, frit

Photo by Roger Schreiber

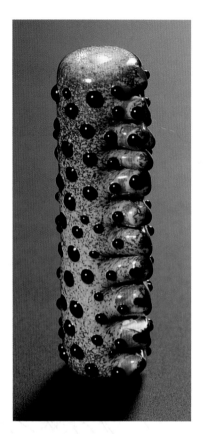

▲ **Hydatina** │ 2006

4.4 x 1.3 x 1.3 cm
Lampworked, trail decorated, cut; soda-
lime glass, enamel, frit,
Photo by Roger Schreiber

▲ **Diamonds** │ 1997

5.7 x 3.2 x 1.3 cm
Lampworked, acid etched;
soda-lime glass
Photo by Roger Schreiber

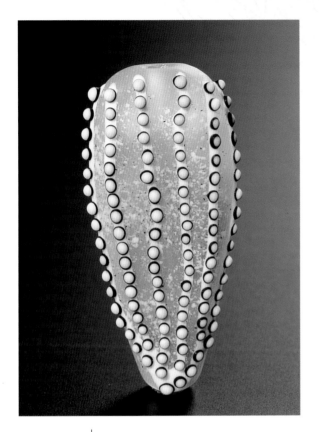

▲ **Sea Fan** | 2002

7 x 3.8 x 1.3 cm
Lampworked, trail decorated,
etched; soda-lime glass, dots
Photo by Roger Schreiber

" People always ask how I can work a full day and then sit down to work on beads at night. Lampworking is a Zen craft. When you are focused and still, things flow easily. It helps me relax. It does not seem like work. "

▲ **Echinoids** | 2003

5.1 x 2.5 x 2.5 cm
Lampworked; frit, engraved
enamel, dots, soda-lime glass
Photo by Roger Schreiber

▲ Metamorphic | 2005

5.1 x 2.2 x 2.2 cm
Lampworked; frit, enamel, dots, soda-lime glass

Photo by Roger Schreiber

" Ancient designs inspire a lot of my work. I spend a
lot of time in museums. Dots are a particular favorite
design of mine—making them modern is always a
challenge. I like their simplicity. "

▲ Untitled | 2006

Left: 2.8 x 2.8 x 2.8 cm; right: 5.1 x 1.6 x
1.6 cm
Lampworked; frit, trail decorated,
enamel, dots, soda-lime glass

Photo by Roger Schreiber

" I have always been interested in tribal cultures and the clues they offer about the present. We aren't as far from our past as we think. Beads are a living reminder of those times. When I sell beads, I like to imagine where they will be hundreds of years from now. "

▲ **Offset Eye Beads** | 2001

    6.4 x 1.9 x 1.9 cm

    Lampworked; dots, soda-lime glass

    Photo by Roger Schreiber

▲ **Modernist** | 2006

    2.2 x 2.2 x 2.2 cm

    Lampworked; trail decorated, dots, soda-lime glass

    Photo by Roger Schreiber

◀ **Tropical Necklace** │ 2000

Each: 2.5 x 2.5 x 1.9 cm; necklace: 45.7 cm
Lampworked, cut; soda-lime glass, enamel
Photo by Roger Schreiber

" When I can't afford a certain bead, making my own is a good alternative. "

▲ Glassmo Necklace | 1999

Each: 4.4 x 1.6 x 1.6 cm; necklace: 61 cm
Lampworked, engraved, etched; soda-lime glass,
polymer clay insets by Cynthia Toops, enamel

Photo by Roger Schreiber

Davide Penso

THE SHOPS AND GALLERIES IN VENICE AND MURANO, ITALY, are filled with beads similar to the kinds travelers would have seen a hundred years ago. The bead-making tradition in Italy is a respected one, but the downside to this respected heritage is that some aspects of the art are slow to change.

Davide Penso embraces the Muranese tradition of glass working, including its tools and techniques, but his pieces stand in sharp contrast to the frilly, adventurine-laden beads of the tourist shops. His pieces are designed to be used in jewelry—primarily in necklaces and bracelets. Penso works quickly and deftly, using shapers and molds that are made for him by toolmakers in Murano. Because his beads aren't stand-alone pieces, they do not demand the technical perfection of elaborate focal beads. A strand of Penso's beads is similar to a corps de ballet: the whole is more than the sum of its parts.

▼ **Solari** | 1999

Each: 5 cm in diameter
Lampworked; Murano glass
Photo by artist

" My involvement with glass has resulted in passion, amusement, and challenge. I don't have the presumption to "work" in glass, but to support it. Glass has molded me. "

◀ Leopardo │ 1995
Each: 1 to 3.5 cm in diameter
Lampworked; Murano glass
Photo by artist

▼ **Minori** | 2000

Each: 1 to 6 cm in diameter
Lampworked; Murano glass
Photo by artist

" Over time, I became keenly interested in learning about
the history and contemporary diversity of glass beads.
Now, I try to explore new avenues of creativity, utilizing
simple, clean lines, and the inspiration of ethnic jewelry. "

DAVIDE PENSO

▲ **Dischi** │ 2005

Each: 6 cm in diameter
Lampworked; Murano glass

Photo by artist

▶ **Tartaruga** │ 1995

Each: 1 to 3 cm in diameter
Lampworked; case beads,
Murano glass

Photo by artist

▲ Conchiglie | 2005
Each: 9 x 2 cm
Lampworked, pulled
strips; Murano glass
Photo by artist

▲ Jacqueline | 2000
Each: 2.2 cm in diameter
Lampworked; gold leaf, Murano glass
Photo by artist

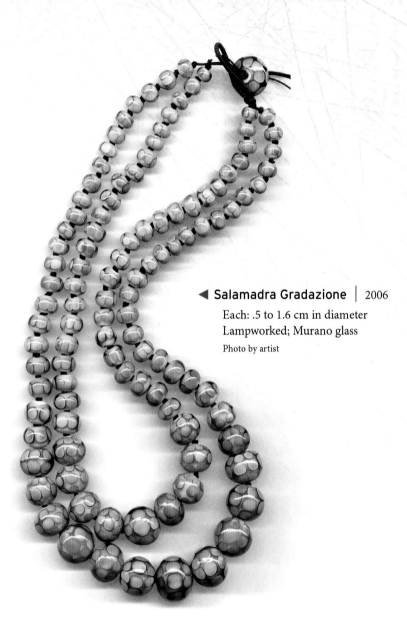

▼ Grige | 2006

Each: 1.2 cm in diameter
Lampworked; cased dots, Murano glass

Photo by artist

◄ Salamadra Gradazione | 2006

Each: .5 to 1.6 cm in diameter
Lampworked; Murano glass

Photo by artist

DAVIDE **PENSO**

" I opened my jewelry studio in Murano, Italy, in 1992, after teaching myself the technique of lampworking. It's not simple to learn a technique, to put yourself on display among the experts, to create something new after centuries of tradition. "

Salamandra | 1998 ▲
Each: 1.6 cm in diameter
Lampworked; Murano glass
Photo by artist

▲ **Desperanza** | 2004
   Each: 4 cm in diameter
   Lampworked; Murano glass
   Photo by artist

▲ **Aligatore** | 1999
   Each: 3 x 2 cm
   Lampworked; dots; Murano glass
   Photo by artist

Doni Hatz

A CAREER IN SCIENTIFIC GLASSBLOWING led Doni Hatz to glass beadmaking. The specialized skills that she learned while making borosilicate laboratory equipment now give her great technical freedom when it comes to creating beads. As with laboratory equipment, most of Hatz's beads begin with clear hollow tubes. She applies stripes of color to a length of tube, then forms a pattern by twisting the tube. Like ships in bottles, small bouquets of flowers bloom inside her hollow bubble beads.

Hatz often uses a complicated technique called encalmo, or montage. This technique involves attaching one striped tube in a perpendicular position to a second tube. When the striped tube is melted down into the second tube, a spiral pattern remains. Encalmo is a difficult process, but Hatz has mastered it, so that her beads are examples of the technique done well.

" Turning points in my work happen when I least expect it. When I'm tired of making the same designs over and over, there's always a moment when time stands still, and the glass flows further than before. Magic appears at the end of the glass rod adding new dots of color, and a new design is born. "

◀ **Untitled** | 1997

4 x 4 x .5 cm
Flameworked, blown, twisted; borosilicate glass tubing, colored glass rods
Photo by Trevor Hart

▲ Spiral Collage | 1997

Each: 5 x 5 x .6 cm
Flameworked, twisted, blown, flattened; borosilicate glass tubing; colored glass rods, incalmo

Photo by Trevor Hart

▲ **Jacketed Floral Bouquet** | 2004

5 x 5 x 5 cm
Flattened, shaped, fused, blown; borosilicate glass
tubing, colored glass rods, millifiori

Photo by Mark Cheadle

" I have worked with both soft glass
and borosilicate. I've experimented
with making larger beads using boro
tubing to envelop a smaller oval-
shaped bead within a larger bead.
I have included individual flowers
that I would seal off inside a bulb.
I'm often asked if the bouquets of
flowers inside the bead are real. "

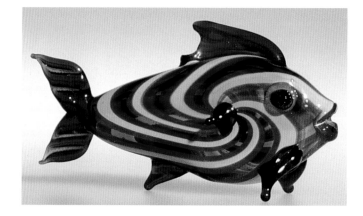

▲ **Spiral Fish** | 1997

2.5 x 6 x .7 cm
Flameworked, blown; twisted; borosilicate glass
tubing, colored glass rods, cobalt glass fins

Photo by Trevor Hart

▲ **Black-Eyed Susan Floral Bouquet** | 1997

5 x 4.5 x 4.5 cm
Flattened and shaped, fused, blown; borosilicate
glass tubing, colored glass rods, millifiori
Photo by Trevor Hart

▲ **Jacketed Floral Bouquet** | 1999

Bead: 5 x 5 x 5 cm; stand: 12 x 10 cm
Cane heated, fused, blown, flattened, shaped, bent; borosilicate glass tubing, colored glass rods, green and dichroic glass
filigrana
Photo by Trevor Hart

◄ **Bead in a Bead** │ 2000

5 x 2.5 x 2.5 cm
Flameworked, striped, blown, twisted, sealed;
borosilicate glass tubing
Photo by Trevor Hart

Untitled │ 1999 ►

4 x 4 x .5 cm
Flameworked, cased, blown, feathered,
flattened; borosilicate glass tubing, colored
glass rods
Photo by Trevor Hart

◀ **Untitled** │ 1999

4 x 4 x .5 cm
Flameworked, cased, feathered, blown,
flattened; borosilicate glass tubing, colored
glass rods

Photo by Trevor Hart

Incalmo Bead │ 1999 ▶

7 x 5 x .7 cm
Flameworked, blown, twisted, fused, flattened;
borosilicate glass tubing incalmo, colored glass
rods, cobalt glass rods, surface decoration

Photo by Trevor Hart

▲ **Amphora Bottle** | 1999

4 x 2.5 x .3 cm
Flameworked, cased, feathered, blown, flattened,
shaped; borosilicate glass tubing, colored glass rods,
cobalt glass rods, cobalt lip and filigrana handles
Photo by Trevor Hart

" Viewing ancient glass in the Corning
Museum of Glass and the Toledo Art
Museum, I saw amphora bottles with the
colors being dragged back and forth. This
inspired me to add new color to classical
designs. I took the technique of feathering
colors one step further to create a new
aspect that had the look of a floral design. "

▲ **Untitled** │ 1997

5 x 5 x .7 cm
Flameworked, blown, twisted; borosilicate
glass tubing, colored glass rods

Photo by Trevor Hart

Shigemichi Yagi

LIKE A BACH KEYBOARD FUGUE, fine lines wind their way in perfect harmony through Shigemichi Yagi's beads. Yagi's lacey, twisted canes are made up of threads of opaque glass suspended in clear glass. When coiled around a core bead, the pattern in the cane oscillates into an hourglass shape.

In the work of many bead makers, simple techniques are manipulated into complex designs on the surface of the bead. In Yagi's work, the complexity comes first. Each of his twisted canes begins with carefully placed opaque lines that are fully encased in clear glass. Once the glass is heated in the torch, the cane is pulled and twisted so that the diameter and rate of rotation is consistent for the length of the cane. If the twist is off-center or the rate of rotation uneven, the even repetitions of pattern in the bead will be disrupted.

◀ **Untitled** │ 1997

2.2 x 3.8 cm
Lampworked, wound on mandrels;
soft glass

Photo by Horigane Yutaka

" I am inspired by a variety of things. When I see a beautiful woman, she gives me a passion to create accessories that are perfect for her. Sometimes watching television will give me an idea for colors. "

▲ **Untitled** | 2006

2.1 x 2 cm
Lampworked, wound on mandrels; soft glass
Photo by Horigane Yutaka

" I learned the traditional Japanese tea ceremony when I was attending university. The wonderful world of that ceremony is part of my aesthetic foundation. "

▲ **Untitled** | 2006
2.5 x 2.2 cm
Lampworked, wound on mandrels; soft glass
Photo by Horigane Yutaka

Untitled | 2006 ▶
2.3 x 2.1 cm
Lampworked, wound on mandrels; soft glass
Photo by Horigane Yutaka

SHIGEMICHI

▲ **Untitled** | 2005

2.2 x 2.2 cm
Lampworked, wound on mandrels;
soft glass

Photo by Horigane Yutaka

Untitled | 2006 ▶

2.7 x 2.4 cm
Lampworked, wound on
mandrels; soft glass

Photo by Horigane Yutaka

▲ **Untitled** | 2005

2.4 x 2.2 cm
Lampworked, wound on mandrels; soft glass
Photo by Horigane Yutaka

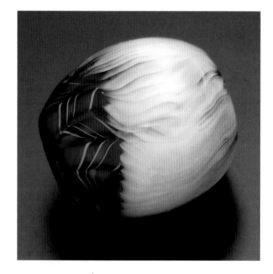

▲ **Untitled** | 2005

2.1 x 2 cm
Lampworked, wound on man-
drels; soft glass
Photo by Horigane Yutaka

▲ **Untitled** │ 2005

    2.5 x 2.1 cm
    Lampworked, wound on mandrels; soft glass

    Photo by Horigane Yutaka

Untitled │ 2005 ▶

    2.2 x 2.1 cm
    Lampworked wound on mandrels;
    soft glass

    Photo by Horigane Yutaka

▲ **Untitled** │ 2006

2.8 x 2.1 cm

Lampworked, wound on mandrels; soft glass

Photo by Horigane Yutaka

" When I first learned how to
work with glass, there were
no books or videos about it
like there are today. It took
me for a long time to figure
out all the techniques and
to understand the natural
properties of the glass. "

▲ **Untitled** │ 2006

2.7 x 2.3 cm
Lampworked, wound on mandrels;
soft glass

Photo by Horigane Yutaka

Bronwen Heilman

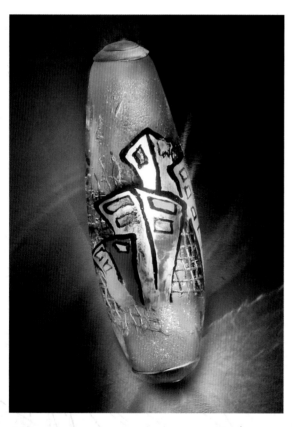

▲ **Escape from the Gated Community** | 2002

6.3 x 2.4 x 2.4 cm
Lampworked; encased copper screen and reverse-painted vitreous enamels, soda-lime glass with a dichroic core, sterling silver endcaps
Photo by Robin Stancliff

GLASS BEADS ARE sometimes described as painterly, but the beads made by Bronwen Heilman are literally painted. The idiosyncratic faces and buildings that float in her beads are painted onto thin sheets of glass. These sheets are heated in a kiln and then carefully wrapped around a core bead that has been prepared in a torch. The painted side of the sheet rests against the surface of the core bead, and the glass sheet serves as a casing layer.

This ingenious technique allows Heilman to incorporate her precise and rather quirky images into long cylinder-shaped beads. Cityscapes, cars, male and female faces, and flowers are all featured in colorful and lively detail in her beads. An accomplished silversmith, Heilman often finishes the beads with sterling tube cores and end caps.

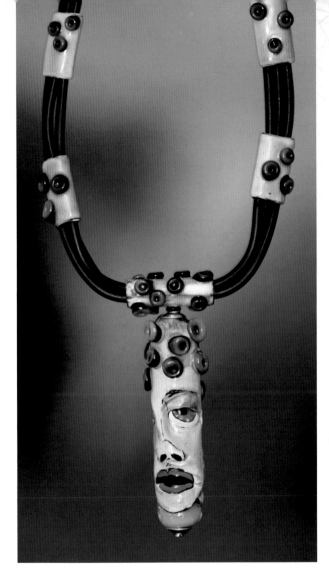

" I will paint an image or sketch on just about anything that stands still for a little while. My influences include big cities—the buildings, the people, the sensation I get walking around. The color of a girl's bicycle spray-painted yellow and orange. The tattoos on bodies. Music—loud, meaningful, and with a strong groove. "

◀ Sarah | 2004

9 x 1.3 x 1.3 cm
Lampworked, sculpted; reverse-painted vitreous enamels, soda-lime glass with a dichroic core, sterling silver end caps, rubber necklace, enameled copper

Photo by Chris Heilman

◀ **Banshee** │ 2002

9 x 1.3 x 1.3 cm
Lampworked; reverse-painted vitreous
enamels, soda-lime glass with a dichroic
core, sterling silver end caps

Photo by Robin Stancliff

Flame Girl │ 2002 ▶

6.5 x 3.8 x 2.4 cm
Lampworked; reverse-painted vitreous
enamels, soda-lime glass with a dichroic
core, sterling silver end caps

Photo by Robin Stancliff

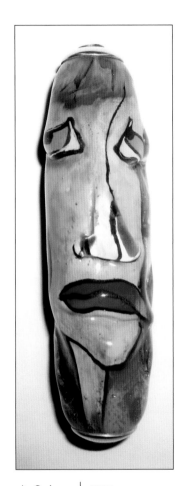

▲ **Colors** | 2004

9 x 2.4 x 2.4 cm
Lampworked, sculpted; soda-
lime glass, reverse-painted
vitreous enamels

Photo by artist

▲ **Car Wreck Shrine** | 2006

15.5 x 20.5 x 4.5 cm
Lampworked; soda-lime glass, reverse-painted vitreous enamels, sterling silver
end caps; stainless steel rods, ancient white heart beads, wood, turquoise, grass

Photo by artist

▲ **Blower Mace** | 2006

    4 x 4 x 1.5 cm
    Lampworked, wound; glass,
    vitreous enamels, pure-gold
    accents, stainless steel bail

    Photo by Robin Stancliff

▲ **Tri-Cut Flower** | 2005

    8 x 2.5 x 1.3 cm
    Lampworked, hand cut, beveled, pol-
    ished; reverse-painted vitreous enam-
    els, soda-lime glass with turquoise core

    Photo by Robin Stancliff

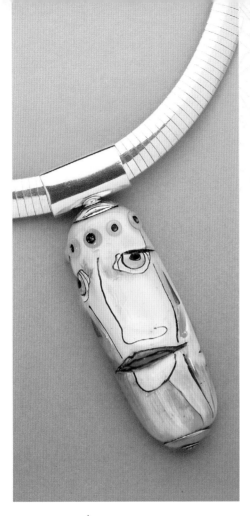

▲ **Untitled** │ 2006

    6.5 x 2.3 x 1.3 cm

    Lampworked, sculpted, cold set, reverse-painted vitreous enamels, soda-lime glass with pink core, sterling silver end caps

    Photo by Robin Stancliff

▲ **Sketch** │ 2006

    3 x 2.3 x 1.5 cm

    Lampworked; soda-lime glass, vitreous enamel on surface, small soda-lime roundels, fine silver, polyester cord

    Photo by Robin Stancliff

◀ **Untitled group** | 1998

Smallest: 3 cm; largest: 4.5 cm
Lampworked; soda-lime glass,
fine silver, stringers, enamels
Photo by artist

" The fluidity of glass as a medium,
the challenges of lampwork
techniques, and the learning
process all drew me to this field. "

" I am always thinking of what else I can do, where I can go with my art. I feel trapped in today, but I always see tomorrow. Tomorrow brings future ideas, future pieces, and a new direction. "

▲ **Untitled** | 1997

Smallest: 2 cm; largest 2 x 2 cm
Lampworked, etched, sandblasted;
soda-lime glass , enamels

Photo by artist

Dustin Tabor

APOLLO AND DIONYSUS EACH HAVE a share in Dustin Tabor's work. Apollo is evident in the clear, clean lines and strong graphic patterns of Tabor's beads, while Dionysus is embodied in their ebullient and surprising color. References to ancient and contemporary beads are frequent in Tabor's work. Tabor also re-examines patterns from Chinese Warring States and Venetian trade beads. He makes simple patterns more complex and explodes color choices as he works.

Tabor makes and applies twisted canes with incredible technical skill. The detail of his dot and pattern work is remarkable. He is the youngest bead maker represented in this book, and his work still displays a youthful compulsion to revel in precision and virtuosity. But there is no doubt about Tabor's ability or his sure-handedness. He makes beads that are ageless.

◀ **Red Murrini Neckpiece** | 2005

Necklace: 47 cm long
Lampworked; manipulated dots, hand-pulled murrini slices, soda-lime glass

Photo by Robert Diamante

Warring States Neckpiece | 2005 ▲

Necklace: 50.8 cm long
Lampworked, dotted, encased; soda-lime glass

Photo by Robert Diamante

▲ **Assorted Warring States Beads with Rosettes** │ 2006

2.5 x 2.3 cm
Lampworked, acid-etched; soda-lime glass, manipulated dots
Photo by Robert Diamante

▲ **Assorted Handmade Beads** | 2004

Each: 2.5 x 2 cm
Lampworked, encased; manipulated dots,
soda-lime glass

Photo by Robert Diamante

Untitled | 2006 ▶

Each: 4.5 x 3.5 cm
Lampworked, layered; manipulated dots, soda-
lime glass

Photo by Robert Diamante

" Glass continues to hold my interest because I never run out of ideas about what I want to create next. I prefer to work as cleanly and simply as possible, using minimal inclusions and basic tools. As a designer obsessed with color, the transparency of glass adds an endless array of possibilities for creating depth and achieving varied tints of color. "

◀ **Bubble-Core Warring States Bead** | 2005

3.2 x 3 cm
Lampworked, encased; manipulated and plunged dots, soda-lime glass

Photo by Robert Diamante

DUSTIN TABOR

◀ **Warring States Bead with Rosettes** | 2005

3.5 x 3.5 cm
Lampworked; manipulated dots, soda-lime glass
Photo by Robert Diamante

Masked Dots & Lines | 2005 ▶

Dimensions unknown
Lampworked; soda-lime glass
Photo by Robert Diamante

◀ **Masked Disc** | 2006

5.5 x 5.5 cm
Lampworked, manipulated, tumbled;
soda-lime glass, overlayed dots

Photo by Robert Diamante

" I'm always astonished at how simple alterations, color variations, and basic manipulations can create an entirely new design. I never try to hide my inspirations. I try to determine what it is about my inspiration that draws me to it, and then infuse this element into my work. "

" As an art student, I was drawn to artists who used strong graphic lines in their work. I think this influence is visible in my own work. I love to combine patterns. A lot of my inspirations for pattern and color combinations have come from textile designs. Talismanic objects, glyphs, runes, and ethnic art also provide inspiration for me. "

▲ **Assorted Pendants** | 2006

Each: 5 x 3.8 cm
Lampworked; manipulated dots, ribbon cane, murrini, soda-lime glass
Photo by Robert Diamante

▲ **Cocoons** | 2006

Smallest: 2.5 x 3 cm
Lampworked, tumbled, etched; soda-lime glass, layered dots
Photo by Robert Diamante

▲ Assorted Pod Forms | 2006

Each: 5.5 x 1.5 cm
Lampworked; layered and manipulated dots and
lines, soda-lime glass

Photo by Robert Diamante

About the Curator

Larry Scott was born in 1947 and has been a full-time bead maker since 1993. His work has been published in *Ornament, Lapidary Journal,* and *Bead & Button* magazines, as well as in *Making Beautiful Beads* and *1000 Glass Beads*, both published by Lark Books. Well known as a teacher and lecturer, Scott frequently teaches in the United States, Canada, Europe, and Japan. He lives in Seattle with his wife, Kathleen Dyer, and a surprising number of cats.

▲ **Larry Scott**
Byzantine Bead | 2007
1.9 x 2.3 x 2.3 cm
Lampworked, heat and gravity shaped, textured, etched, dichroic coating; soda-lime glass
Photo by Andrea Guarino-Slemmons

Acknowledgments

I want to thank the following for their help and suggestions: Michael Barley, Andrea Guarino-Slemmons, Diana East, Jim Jones, Lani Ching, Kristina Logan, Kate Fowle Meleney, Leah Fairbanks, Jim Kervin, Bronwen Heilman, Pat Frantz, Jim Berry, and Katherine Wadsworth.

Joanie Beldin was generous in her support of photography for this book. Special thanks to Morio Toyoshima of Studio Morio and Kyonobu Miyamoto of the Kobe Lampwork Museum in Japan for help with communication and translation. Suzanne Tourtillott and Shannon Quinn-Tucker were always patient. They must have had practice.

And thanks, of course, to Kathleen Dyer, my wife of 29 years, who said, "Do you really want to do this? Everyone will hate you." To which I replied, "But there will be 40 bead makers who think I have exquisite taste." As always, she gave me her full support, despite her better judgment.

Though some were overused, no adjectives or adverbs were actually harmed in the writing of this book. Nouns and verbs are another matter.

—*Larry Scott*

Artists' Biographies

Dan Adams

Adams has been showing his glass work in dozens of museums and galleries throughout the world since 1993, including the American Craft Museum, the Finnish Glass Museum, the Musée du Verre, and the Ceramics and Folk Craft Museum in Toyota City, Japan. Well-known for his engraved enamel beads, he has also appeared in *Lapidary Journal*, *Ornament*, and *The Complete Book of Glass Beadmaking* (Lark Books, 2005), among others.

Michael Barley

Barley was a potter for 15 years, but, once introduced to the art, he was immediately captivated by glass bead making. He enjoys experimenting with color, shape, texture, and technique and creating unique designs. Barley occasionally teaches at his home studio and throughout the United States.

Tom Boylan

A self-taught artist who has been creating beads for over 20 years, Boylan focuses on quality rather than quantity to produce unique, detailed, handmade glass beads. While he mixes some of his own colors, he purchases the rest from commercial manufacturers in order to focus time on making his beads. Boylan's work can be found in bead stores and at bead shows across the nation.

Harold Williams Cooney

A glass artist in Manchester, New Hampshire, Cooney has been doing lampworking for the past seven years.

Lark Dalton and Corrie Haight

Haight and Dalton both studied glassworking at Pilchuck Glass School, and today have their own studio where they create hand-blown glass beads and other glass art. Their work has been represented at museums and shows across the globe—including the Bulles de Perles in Sars Poteries, France—and Dalton has assisted in teaching several workshops in the United States. The pair has also been featured in magazines such as *Bead & Button*, *Lapidary Journal*, and *Ornament*.

Pam Dugger

Having worked with glass since 1974, Dugger started glass bead making in 1988. Within a few years she had developed a way of creating hollow glass beads in order to form natural-looking fish and birds. She has taught regionally and nationally, but in the future will focus her teaching at her studio, River of Glass. Dugger's work is featured in galleries across the United States, as well as in several magazines and books.

Diana East

East worked as a freelance jewelry designer for 20 years before she began to work with glass in 1995. She has since taught throughout the United States and Europe. East's work is featured in Lomas Gallery and New Ashgate Gallery in the United Kingdom, and Morgan Contemporary Glass Gallery in the United States; she also has work in permanent collections in the Musée de France, the Museo del Vidrio, and the Bead Museum in Washington, D.C. She has been featured in the publications *Lapidary Journal, Beads of Glass* (Pyro Press, 2003), and *1000 Glass Beads* (Lark Books, 2004).

Leah Fairbanks

Fairbanks started working with glass in 1982; her first bead-making class was 10 years later. Since then, she has been involved in promoting professional lampwork glass bead making, serving on the Board of Directors of the International Society of Glass Beadmakers, and teaching advanced workshops throughout the world, including at Red Deer College. She has also been a presenter at the Annual Japanese Bead Festival, and *Bead & Button* honored her with a commission for a commemorative glass bead. Fairbanks was one of the first American artists to incorporate Japanese Satake glass in her work, and her use of garden motifs has influenced floral decoration within contemporary glass bead making. Her work is featured in galley shows around the world.

Pat Frantz

After studying art at California State University, Long Beach, and earning a Masters in sculptural ceramics, Frantz was introduced to lampworking at the Pilchuck Glass School. Her work has been exhibited in the United States, Europe, and Japan, as well as featured in publications such as *Collectible Beads* (Ornament, 1995), *Contemporary Lampworking* (Salusa Glassworks, 1997), and *Making Glass Beads* (Lark Books, 2004). Frantz teaches at various locations throughout the year, and she also has her own instructional beadmaking videos.

Andrea Guarino-Slemmons

Guarino-Slemmons began working with stained glass while she was a teenager, and from there eventually moved to lampworking. Since then, she has focused primarily on making glass beads, experimenting with various metal foils and chemicals to create reactions in the glass. Guarino-Slemmons teaches at her studio, as well as around the nation and world, and her work has been featured in newspapers and magazines such as *Bead & Button*.

Doni Hatz

Hatz is a scientific and artistic glassblower. She began to apply her experience with the art of precision work to glass beads, goblets, and sculpture. While still fabricating scientific glassware for research and development, she continues to pursue her passion with glass art. Her work has been published in the magazine *Fusion* and in various books such as *Contemporary Lampworking* (Salusa Glassworks, 2002), *Formed of Fire* (Salusa Glassworks, 2003), *1000 Glass Beads* (Lark Books, 2004), and *500 Glass Objects* (Lark Books, 2006).

Hiroko Hayashi-Kogure

Hayashi-Kogure first started lampworking in 1995, learning the art of beadmaking without formal education. A few years later she began to exhibit at various shows, and soon afterwards began teaching workshops. She learned the art of core glass from her husband and has received an award from the National Small Bonsai Association for her work in that area. Her work has also been featured in publications such as *1000 Glass Beads* (Lark Books, 2004), *Contemporary Glass Beads by 30 Japanese Artists* (Ribun Shuppan, 2004), and *Beads of Glass* (Pyro Press, 2003).

Bronwen Heilman

A glass artist since 1996, Heilman looks forward to working with glass every day. She teaches beginning and intermediate glass bead making classes and has presented workshops on how to sandblast beads. Her work is shown in several galleries in the United States, including Abington Art Center and the Museum of Glass in Tacoma, Washington. Heilman has been featured in a number of publications, such as *Glass Craftsman* magazine, *1000 Glass Beads* (Lark Books, 2004), and *Bronwen Heilman: Vitreous Painting Techniques for Glass Beadmaking* (GlassWear Studios, 2005).

Sage Holland

Sage Holland became an apprentice under master beadmaker Brian Kerkvliet in 1987, after many years of working in various other fine arts, and soon afterwards started her own studio, focusing on lampworking. Since then she has been called one of the American glass bead making pioneers, and her work has been shown in several magazines and books, as well as exhibitions across the globe. Along with her husband, Tom Holland, Sage teaches workshops nationally and internationally.

Tom Holland

Tom Holland first became interested in beads as a child and after receiving two degrees in fine arts, began to pursue his desire to make beads. He first began glass bead making in 1990 and has since been featured in numerous publications, including the magazines *Ornament*, *Lapidary Journal*, and *Bead & Button*. Tom is also credited with helping to rediscover the creation process of some of history's most intriguing beads: beads from the Chinese warring states, as well as the Islamic era folded glass beads. He frequently presents at conferences and seminars, as well as teaching throughout the world.

James Allen Jones

Jones started bead making in 1987, teaching himself through trial and error. Inspired by the work of Japanese beadmaker Kyoyo Asao, he began to develop a cold bundling technique for creating mosaic cane using a small glass furnace. Today he continues to refine this process while making lampwork beads of many styles, including intricate mosaic glass beads. His work has been shown in national and international exhibitions, as well as publications such as *Bead & Button*, *Jewelry Craft*, *Beads of Glass* (Pyro Press, 2003), and *1000 Glass Beads* (Lark Books, 2004). Jones also teaches his craft at various shows throughout the world.

Norikazu Kogure

Kogure graduated from Toyama Glass Art Institute in 1994, and a year later started his own studio. He has since been a demonstrator at numerous conferences and exhibitions, including the Taiwan International Glass Exhibition, as well as an instructor at Musashino Art College. Kogure's work may be found in several publications, including *Contemporary Glass Beads by 20 Japanese Artists* (Ribun Shuppan, 2000), *Contemporary Lampworking* (Salusa Glassworks, 2002), and *1000 Glass Beads* (Lark Books, 2004).

Kristina Logan

Logan's work can be found in numerous galleries—including Aaron Faber Gallery, Musée-Atelier du Verre, and Renwick Gallery of the Smithsonian American Art Museum—as well as publications such as *Lapidary Journal*, *Beadwork*, and *1000 Glass Beads* (Lark Books, 2004). She is also an exhibitor at several shows and teaches beadmaking workshops.

Bruce St. John Maher

Inspired by his grandparents, Maher learned to work with glass by studying ancient techniques and through experimentation. He applies details by hand to each piece, and his private collections have gained national recognition. His work has appeared in several publications, including *Bead & Button*, *Making Bead and Wire Jewelry* (Lark Books, 2002), and *The Painted and Faceted Fused Beads of Bruce St. John Maher* (GlassWear Studios, 2004).

Toshimasa Masui

Masui began lampworking in 1987 without receiving any formal education in the art, and six years later opened his own studio in Japan. Since 1994 he has taught at several different establishments, and served as judge at lampworking competitions. His work has been featured at art galleries throughout Japan, and he has also demonstrated at shows in the United States.

Kate Fowle Meleney

Meleney started taking glass bead making workshops in 1991. A year later she began teaching workshops in flameworked bead making at her own studio, as well as at other locations around the world. Her work has been featured in numerous magazines, such as *Lapidary Journal*, and books, including *The Enamel and Electroform Decorated Beads of Kate Fowle Meleney* (GlassWear Studios, 2002), and *1000 Glass Beads* (Lark Books, 2004). Meleney has also made instructional videos in beadmaking.

Donna Milliron

As a glass artist, Milliron is known for her pâte de verre beads and sculptures, as well as her fused, flameworked, and raku beads. Her work can be seen nationwide in bead stores, catalogs, galleries, and museums. With her husband, she also runs Arrow Springs, a flameworking supply manufacturer, and The Springs, a school that hosts workshops by leading glassworkers.

Gail Crosman Moore

The common denominator in all of Moore's work is her passion for creating, no matter what the material. She loves color, form, and texture, and wants her work to bring joy to its audience. Gail can often be found at shows and workshops throughout North America, exhibiting and teaching.

Mary Mullaney and Ralph Mossman

The husband and wife team of Mossman and Mullaney are known for their skill in glassblowing. Working together since 1985, they create unique and complex contemporary glassworks that demonstrate the couple's dedication to fine hand-blown glass. They have taught workshops throughout the United States, and exhibited at shows across the globe. They have collections at the Lightner Museum and the Glendale Bead Museum. Mossman and Mullaney have also won several awards—including the Idaho Governor's Award for Excellence in the Arts—and been featured in numerous publications, such as *Collectible Beads* (Ornament, 1995) and *American Craft*.

Akihiro Ohkama

Ohkama began studying glass bead making under his father in 1996. He soon opened his own studio and shop in Nara, Japan. He strives to create realistic patterns and expressions, and he wants his art to express not only Japanese culture, but other areas of the world as well. Ohkama has been an exhibitor in shows throughout the world, and his work has been published in several books, including *Beads of Glass* (Pyro Press, 2003) and *1000 Glass Beads* (Lark Books, 2004).

Kristen Frantzen Orr

Orr combines her love of nature with her artistic skills in watercolor to create unique, handmade glass beads. Her detailed work includes using canes from multiple colors of glass combined with transparent colors to produce a captivating play of light. Orr's work can be seen throughout the United States, as well as Japan, England, South Africa, and Australia. She has also been featured in magazines and books such as *GLASS*, *Ornament*, and *Bead Art* (Kalmbach, 1998).

Karen Ovington

Ovington began flameworking in 1994, and since then she has been an exhibitor and teacher at several shows and workshops. She has been featured in numerous publications, including *Contemporary Lampworking* (Salusa Glassworks, 1997), *Making Glass Beads* (Lark Books, 2004), and *500 Beaded Objects* (Lark Books, 2004). Ovington's work is also on display at Arts Afire Glass Gallery, Mindscape Adornments, and the Highland Park Art Center.

Davide Penso

Self-taught in the art of lampworking, Penso opened his own studio in Murano, Italy, in 1992. Under the instruction of his future father-in-law, he learned to make mosaic and gold-leafed beads. Since then, Penso has continued to explore the creative possibilities of bead making, incorporating simple lines and ethnic jewelry. His work has been shown in museums such as Venice's Museo Correr, the Glass Museum of Murano, and Boston's Fine Arts Museum. Penso also teaches private classes at his studio.

Sharon Peters

Doodling and designing since she was young, Peters studied art at the University of California, Irvine, and eventually began creating glassworks for commissions. She was first introduced to glass bead making in 1996, and she began to incorporate her cartoon drawings from earlier years to create sculptural beads. Peters is a frequent participant at exhibits throughout the world, and has been featured in several magazines, such as *Bead & Button*, and books, including *1000 Glass Beads* (Lark Books, 2004).

René Roberts

Roberts studied at Pilchuck Glass School, and since 1983 has been showing her art at museums and exhibits around the world, including the Boston Society of Arts and Crafts, the Ceramics and Folk Craft Museum in Toyota City, Japan, and the Glass Museum in Ebeltoft, Denmark. Roberts is also the inventor of a coloring process used with metal leaf and oxides on the surface of the glass. Her work can be seen in *Making Glass Beads* (Lark Books, 1997), *Formed of Fire* (Salusa Glassworks, 2003), and *Lapidary Journal*, among other publications.

Emiko Sawamoto

Sawamoto fell in love with glass art when she visited Italy in 1995. After trying a few forms of glass art classes, she found glass bead making to be her forte and, with no official art training, set up her own studio the same year. Primarily a bead maker, Sawamoto started to make small lampworked sculptures in 1998. Her work has been exhibited internationally, and she helps Japanese artists and galleries to communicate with American and European lampworkers for exhibitions and events. Sawamoto's art has also been in several publications, such as *Making Beautiful Beads* (Lark Books, 2002), *Formed of Fire* (Salusa Glassworks, 2003), and *Beads of Glass* (Pyro Press, 2003).

Terri Caspary Schmidt

Schmidt first discovered lampworking in 1999. Her work is inspired by the patterns and forms of nature, as well as the drawings of biologist Ernst Haeckel and the photographs of Karl Blossfeldt. In 2004 she won second place in the *Lapidary Journal* Bead Arts Award. Schmidt's work may be seen in various publications, such as *1000 Glass Beads* (Lark Books, 2004) and *The Complete Book of Glass Beadmaking* (Lark Books, 2005).

Yoshiko Shiiba

Shiiba began creating glass art in 1978, and since then has been closely involved in several glass bead events. She has taught workshops and courses, coordinated exhibitions and festivals, as well as judged the Beads Grand Prix. Her work has also been displayed in several solo and group exhibitions throughout Japan.

James Smircich

Smircich first apprenticed at the Nourot glass studio in Benicia, California, in 1979. He went on to marble making and cane making. He is a founding member of the International Society of Glass Beadmakers, and he now teaches classes worldwide and gives private lessons in Eugene, Oregon.

Loren Stump

Stump began working with glass in molten form in 1993. Self-taught, he is known for an innovative technique that manipulates a two-dimensional murrine slice into a three-dimensional form. Stump is a well-known instructor and teaches throughout the United States and the world. His work has been featured at the Corning Museum of Glass, the Ertz Israel Museum, and the Kyokei Fujita Glass Museum.

Dustin Tabor

After beginning to make beads in 1996, Tabor eventually found his way to lampworking. He soon established his own studio and began experimenting with the art, discovering his own sense of color. Tabor's work is known for its technical precision and his contemporary interpretation of ancient bead patterns. His teaches throughout the United States, and his work has been featured in galleries such as Arts Afire Glass Gallery and Symmetry Gallery, as well as the magazines *Bead & Button*, *Beadwork*, and *Lapidary Journal*.

Toshiki Uchida

A glass artist in Kawaguchi, Japan, Uchida has studied at the Tokyo Glass Art Institute and taught at the Joshibi University of Art and Design. His work has been featured in numerous solo exhibitions in Japan and in other exhibitions around the world.

Pati Walton

Fascinated by glass as a child, Walton first began working with stained glass in 1979. Thirteen years later, she started lampworking, teaching herself the art. She is known for the nature and aquarium scenes she incorporates into her beads, as well as her specialty of making murrine. Walton teaches several classes every year throughout the world, and her work has been featured in numerous exhibits and publications across the globe, including the Madrid Art Gallery Exhibit, *Jewelry Crafts*, and *Beads of Glass* (Pyro Press, 2003).

Shigemichi Yagi

Yagi first began working with glass in 1983, creating stained glass art. Seven years later, he learned lampworking and eventually opened a studio. Exhibiting throughout Japan, he had also had work that appeared in publications such as Contemporary *Glass Beads by 30 Japanese Artists* (Ribun Shuppan, 2004).

Nicole Zumkeller and Eric Seydoux

Seydoux and Zumkeller tumbled into glass bead making after meeting some of the pioneers of the American glass bead renaissance. Since 1995, the pair have been full-time bead makers, teaching several classes every year at various locations in Europe. They have been exhibitors at galleries and shows throughout the world, such as the Los Angeles Craft & Folk Art Museum. They have also been published in several magazines, newspapers, and books, including *1000 Glass Beads* (Lark Books, 2004).

Artist Index